"*Soul Hunger* is good news for anyone tired of temporary gratification that leaves a bitter aftertaste. Prepare yourself for the kind of mouthwatering nourishment you were made to enjoy."

—KURT BRUNER, author of *Why Isn't God Nice?* and *It Starts at Home*

"As I began to read *Soul Hunger* I was fascinated by the concept of the book. The more I read, the more I was personally challenged to examine my actions, my decisions, my desires, and my heart. I'll be the first to admit that self-examination is not my favorite afternoon activity, but as I continued to read I became convinced it would be worth the effort. With highlighter in hand, I left my mark on page after page. And my conclusion? Reading *Soul Hunger*, digesting its content and concepts, can lead to life changes that will feed your soul and honor God."

—KENDRA SMILEY, national and international speaker and author of several books, including *Live Free: Eliminate the If Onlys and What Ifs of Life*

"If you are struggling with control, worry, insecurity, or feel trapped in habitual sins, perhaps you are battling deep idols in your soul. With great clarity and intriguing biblical illustrations, Otis explains how these destroying heart issues can be exchanged for God's peace and genuine soul satisfaction. *Soul Hunger* is not a self-change manual but rather a captivating encounter of how God can change any heart if we choose to let Him. Go from dreaming about how you want your life to be to living with God fulfilling your deepest longings. Grab a pen, and curl up on the couch; let God begin filling your soul with genuine beauty and peace as you read."

—SHARON HOFFMAN, conference speaker and author of six books, including *There's a Car Seat in My Convertible* and *The G.I.F.T.ed Woman*

"With great clarity, simplicity, and a heart for God, J. Otis Ledbetter, in *Soul Hunger*, meets a great need in life today. Far too often a new book comes out and there is very little that is helpful to the deep spiritual longings of life. This book is different. Every chapter is rich, understandable, and helpful. I appreciated how topics like happiness and truth were broken down and explained, and each chapter could be used for group and personal study."

—DR. MARK MILIONI, president, Baptist Bible College and Theological Seminary

"What an incredibly refreshing treatment of an unpleasant topic! No one enjoys being hungry, but J. Otis Ledbetter provides a rich feast of truth to satisfy the hunger we all possess within. Not only does the author share deep and insightful truths concerning each of the 'hungers' he deals with in each chapter—he fills each chapter with rich illustrations from both life and literature. You will be both challenged and blessed to find ways to satisfy your many hungers. In addition, the appendix is worth the price of the book!"

—BOB BURNEY, president and founder of CrossPower Ministries and host of *Bob Burney Live* on WRFD Radio, the Salem Media affiliate in Columbus, Ohio

"Practical and compelling! Dr. Ledbetter skillfully unveils what often troubles our souls and derails our lives. *Soul Hunger* unleashes the practical power to fearlessly confront any confusion and disease that may be found at the root of everyday choices."

—VIRGINIA DIXON, director of inner healing, Center for New Medicine and Cancer Center for Healing

# SOUL HUNGER

{ *Satisfy Your Heart's Deepest Longing* }

J. OTIS LEDBETTER

NEW HOPE®
PUBLISHERS
Imprint of Iron Stream Media

BIRMINGHAM, ALABAMA

New Hope® Publishers
5184 Caldwell Mill Rd.
St. 204-221
Hoover, AL 35244
NewHopePublishers.com
An imprint of Iron Stream Media

Library of Congress Cataloging-in-Publication Data

Names: Ledbetter, J. Otis, author.
Title: Soul hunger : satisfy your heart's deepest longing / J. Otis Ledbetter.
Description: First [edition]. | Birmingham : New Hope Publishers, 2019.
Identifiers: LCCN 2019010772 | ISBN 9781563091513 (permabind)
Subjects: LCSH: Fruit of the Spirit. | Bible. Galatians, V, 22-23—Criticism,
    interpretation, etc. | Christian life. | Soul—Christianity.
Classification: LCC BV4501.3 .L43 2019 | DDC 234/.13—dc23
LC record available at https://lccn.loc.gov/2019010772

ISBN-13: 978-1-56309-151-3
Ebook ISBN: 978-1-56309-152-0

1 2 3 4 5—23 22 21 20 19

My wife Gail and I, with the fervent prayer of hope, dedicate this book to our next generation. To Riley Nicole, Madalyn Rose, Abigail Grace, Ashley Brooke, Lauren Joy, Lillian Joy, Samantha Gail, Alexandria Jane, Cassidy Faith, Alexis Faith, Jack Thomas, and James Fenton.

To our grandchildren . . . may you turn to the fruit of the Spirit to satisfy every hunger pang you ever encounter in the course of your beautiful lives! In the imperfection of our earthly lives we pray that through your grandparents and parents you find the perfect peace that remains beyond all understanding!

---

# CONTENTS

Hardly a day has passed this last year that someone special to this project hasn't come into my mind. People like my wife Gail and my executive secretary Sherry, who have nurtured and protected the intellectual property contained on these pages in myriad ways. When the proposal was almost ready to deliver to my literary agent, Bob Hostetler of the Steve Laube agency, who held my feet to the fire to make the manuscript "sing" for potential readers, Thomas Womack carved out a week during the 2018 holiday season to use his editor's knowhow to help make the notes on the pages fit the melody. Friend and fellow author Steve Van Winkle added research, stories, and his writing skills to help fill in places where reinforcement was needed. Then when Ramona Richards of New Hope Publishers read the proposal and decided to give it a go, the die had been cast. Now it all comes together in what I believe to be a beautifully architected manuscript, aided by these professionals, to place into the reader's hands information I believe has the potential to change lives.

And I so hope it might do that for you.

# CHAPTER 1

# EVERYBODY'S HUNGRY FOR SOMETHING

W hen's the last time you were hungry? Truly hungry? Was it painful? Did you feel a tightness or contraction in your stomach? Were you dizzy or faint? Agitated or irritable?

This is when you realize hunger isn't a weakness—it's a force! It allows no time to think of anything except the gnawing desire for food.

This force drives a street person to rummage through trashcans. For the homeless or indigent, hunger is a brutal master.

That scenario takes me to a familiar story in the Bible about a wasteful son who asked for and received his inheritance from his father. He then recklessly spent it all. With everything desirable to eat then out of reach, he was forced to turn to what was available—carob pods the swine were eating (Luke 15:11–32).

If hunger's cruel pangs have hammered your belly, you know how it can drive you to do almost anything, to act in ways you never thought you would. Victor Hugo illustrated this in *Les Misérables* when hunger pushed Jean Valjean to steal a single loaf of bread, resulting in a lifetime of agony and danger.

Thankfully, few of us are acquainted with that degree of chronic hunger, the kind that claws at your belly, assaults your mind, and refuses to let go. But

*At birth, each of us possesses God-given hungers, which we spend our lives trying to gratify.*

we all know a different kind of hunger, one that's universal. It tells and retells how our souls crave something far deeper and more important than physical food. At birth, each of us possesses God-given hungers, which we spend our lives trying to gratify. They gnaw at our psyche, begging to be satisfied. Though we may not be able to name any such hunger, it dogs us.

Everybody is hungry for . . . *something.*

It's there in our alone moments. When we lay our head on our pillow at night, when we finally have a moment to think, we sense it—a deep longing for intimacy, a lack of contentment, an anxious appetite for some kind of control, or a hunger for truth. It may stem from something in our past, from something yet unfulfilled, or from something lost in previous experiences.

Maybe you're presently seeking to satisfy a suppressed hunger you may not yet fully realize is there. You've sensed something out of balance in your life. That imbalance causes you to look deeper within. In doing so honorably, you may begin uncovering layer after layer of your complex inability to sustain a steady spiritual walk. You've tried everything—money, new relationships, travel, a new job. Maybe you're making some fresh endeavor this very moment. Because down deep, things aren't all together. You find yourself hustled about by dissonance in your reality.

Well, you're not alone.

In trying to satisfy our hungers, we realize something eludes us, something we haven't clearly understood. Life gets so blurred with daily tasks big and small that in our busyness, we haven't found time to discover sufficient sustenance for an acceptable spiritual path to satiate our hungers. We may be driven to countless trips to our spiritual cupboards, endlessly scrounging. We may feel destined to search forever without finding anything.

> *In our delay to discovering some legitimate pathway to satisfaction, we'll often succumb to temptation and sin.*

In our delay to discovering some legitimate pathway to satisfaction, we'll often succumb to temptation and sin. Then comes confusion, a feeling of spiritual failure, of disheartenment and defeat.

Yet the whisper still tells us: *You are hungry.*

## TWO LISTS—ONE TALE

In an ancient letter written two thousand years ago to a people known as Galatians, two lists are embedded. Each list describes characteristics that are within the reach of human experience. One list speaks of good qualities, the other of aberrant behavior. One offers the best of times, the other the worst of times. After reading both, one list leaves us with a sense of inspiring freshness, the other the stench of a garbage pail.

Here's one list the author wrote: "The fruit of the Spirit is love, joy, peace, longsuffering, kindness, goodness, faithfulness, gentleness, self-control" (Galatians 5:22–23). To scan over these characteristics elicits no fear, dredges up no past, and creates no emotional baggage. In fact, the author goes on to write, "Against such there is no law" (v. 23). There are no laws, whether national or local, that control the fruit of the Spirit. That's because no laws are needed to impede the flow of such goodness from relationship to relationship.

All the laws on the books are, by contrast, made to impede the flow of what the author calls the manifestations of the flesh. Listen to his listing of these: "Now the works of the flesh are evident, which are: adultery, fornication, uncleanness, lewdness, idolatry, sorcery, hatred, contentions, jealousies, outbursts of wrath, selfish ambitions, dissensions, heresies, envy, murders, drunkenness, revelries, and the like" (vv. 19–21).

Any inspiring words there?

Hardly! Seems like just a pile of debris running over with human wreckage.

One day in my office with an open Bible, I made a list of these works of the flesh juxtaposed to the fruit of the Spirit. I wrote them on large sticky notes and placed them on the wall opposite my desk. For days, I studied them to find answers to such questions as these: Why is anger only found in the works of the flesh? Where would that square with anger's antithesis—with what the Spirit produces? (In full disclosure, I tried to squeeze anger into a component of the fruit of the Spirit.)

Over time, after daily meditation on the two lists, clarity began to emerge. I began to see that the fruit of the Spirit was given to satisfy human hungers placed in us by God in a fashion benefiting everyone, while the works of the flesh—created by and strongly suggested by Satan—were only substitutes for what God intended us to experience.

One list satisfies the eternal; the other is entirely temporal.

The difference between the eternal and the temporal began to grow clear for me; in fact, I'd read about it countless times before in the Bible. This difference is seen in various lives chronicled throughout Scripture and finally articulated by John in the last book, Revelation. He describes a vision in which an angel presents him with a scroll and tells him to eat it: "Then I took the little book out of the angel's hand and ate it, and it was as sweet as honey in my mouth. But when I had eaten it, my stomach became bitter" (Revelation 10:10).

John here relates the strange scene of eating a scroll, or small book. While the details of that account aren't important for us here, the experience of eating this little scroll illustrates the essential difference—and deceptive similarities—between the fruit of the Spirit and the works of the flesh.

Initially, John said this book tasted like honey. Not many of us eat bowls of honey today, but in John's day, this was the equivalent of eating a candy bar. However, his sweet treat hadn't run its full course.

Once eaten, the scroll turned his stomach bitter. Here is the long-term effect, the lasting problem from a moment's pleasure. We've probably all experienced this kind of regret. Maybe we simply ate too much of a good thing, or maybe that egg salad sat a day too long in the fridge. In either case, what tasted so wonderful began to wreak havoc on our digestive tract.

If we could know from the taste of food how good or bad it would be for us in the long run, we might all be a little healthier. And make better choices.

This is where John's account relates to our concerns.

The fruit of the Spirit and the works of the flesh are the choices set before us. Initially, both are like John's little scroll in that they taste sweet—they both seem to effectively satisfy. This is the deception. The real danger in the works of the flesh can't be discerned by their initial taste but only in the bitter after-effect they have on us and the people in our lives. Only then do we understand what a mistake we made in consuming them.

This is where we discover that one list represents the real, the other the unreal. The fruit of the Spirit is the real and true sugar; the works of the flesh is the saccharin (unreal, imitation). Although both lists promise pleasure and satisfaction to fulfill the same hunger, each list produces different long-term results. One is sweet to the taste and genuinely satisfying. The other is like John's little scroll—initially sweet, but leaving a lasting, bitter aftertaste.

Here's how the list on my wall looked as it began to take shape.

| The Works of the Flesh | The Fruit of the Spirit |
|---|---|
| Adultery | Love |
| Fornication | |
| Uncleanness | Joy |
| Lewdness/Licentiousness | |
| Idolatry | Peace |
| Sorcery | |
| Hatred | Longsuffering |
| Contention | |
| Jealousy | Kindness |
| Anger | |
| Selfish Ambition | Goodness |
| Dissension | |
| Heresy | Faithfulness |
| Envy | Gentleness |
| Murder | |
| Drunkenness | Self-Control/Temperance |
| Revelry | |

I studied these two lists for so long I thought my eyes might become permanently crossed. The two lists seemed to be opposites with some great impassable gulf fixed between them. Yet they matched—not like identical twins, but more like a celebrity look-alike. For instance, love versus adultery and fornication. In our society, don't people call adultery or fornication "making love"? Or joy versus uncleanness and lewdness. Don't we equate uncleanness and lewd behavior as some sort of joy, even if only a cheap thrill? So when each as a hunger buster has us in its grip, we aren't seeking a definition—just satisfaction. Each of the above has the potential to do just that, even if only temporarily.

Obviously the two lists were fundamentally different, yet I observed what seemed to me to be startling parallels.

## YEARNINGS THAT CREATE HUNGER

I attended a men's conference not long ago where one of the guest speakers was an amazing presidential look-alike. When he spoke, he sounded like the president, and he dressed like the president. His routine was so impressive I found myself forgetting he really wasn't the president; I had a hard time convincing my mind he was actually a fake.

This is the kind of parallel of which I'm speaking. For some people, seeing love listed alongside adultery or fornication seems natural enough. To a child of God, the difference is stark. But to the man not thinking spiritually, love, adultery, and fornication may resemble each other quite remarkably. It's easy to see how such a mistake could be made by the sensual mind—a mind that sees things through the low light of a shady world.

In addition to that natural tendency is another dynamic: the presence and activity of the evil one, the enemy of souls, the one the Bible calls Satan. He's the ultimate celebrity look-alike. Created as an angel of light, he now masquerades as the Father of lights! His assignment is to lure us to the replica and make it appear enchantingly real.

Sitting at the desk with my eyes fixed on the two lists on my office wall, I received more clarity. I recognized that both offer answers. Those answers correspond to the questions most humans are asking. They represent the alleviation of hungers we experience for things like connection, intimacy, happiness, peace, and truth.

The lists on the wall offered solutions—as well as insight into the contest between real and unreal, seen and unseen, eternal and temporal.

The wrappings of human flesh contain yearnings that must be satisfied. There are remedies for every human hunger. In his book *Mere Christianity*, C. S. Lewis reasons, "Creatures are not born with desires unless satisfaction for those desires exist. A baby feels hunger: well, there is such a thing as food. . . . Men feel sexual desire: well, there is such a thing as sex." Remedies for human hungers are sometimes complicated. Not just any liquid can assuage thirst; liquid antifreeze resembles fruit juice, but it's best not to drink it! Hunger cannot be satisfied by just any rations; the mushrooms in your yard may look like those in the grocery store, but don't go slicing them up for your vegetable soup this evening! And I'll never forget when I saw the pretty, green, unripe apples hanging across the fence from my neighbor's yard. They looked so inviting. Though I was warned by a caring mom not to eat them, I discovered the turmoil they can bring to a youngster's digestive track.

There's a righteous prescription for every soul hunger. But there's also an *unrighteous* resolution.

That's our problem.

Even the most casual look into our culture will tell you that the unrighteous resolution is at first glance the most attractive. As A. W. Tozer writes in *The Root of the Righteous*, "The bias of nature is toward the wilderness, never toward the fruitful field."[1] Our natural tendencies lean toward the unrighteous.

The two lists on my office wall represent the righteous and unrighteous ways to relieve the many hungers of our soul. The true Father of lights has made the righteous ways available through the ministry of the Holy Spirit, but the great masquerader—the celebrity look-alike—has provided almost twice as many unrighteous ways.

*There's a righteous prescription for every soul hunger. But there's also an unrighteous resolution.*

As I studied those two lists and saw that each side brings resolution for particular human hungers (although only temporarily on one side), I realized a third list was needed.

I stuck another large sheet of paper on the wall between the original lists and began to write:

- Intimacy
- Happiness
- Contentment
- Justice
- Control
- Respect
- Truth
- Achievement
- Pleasure

A matrix began to take shape, and the light of Scripture began to illuminate my heart and mind. I began to appreciate that what was on the wall was the emergence

---

1. A. W. Tozer, *The Root of the Righteous* (Chicago: Moody Publishers, 2015). Accessed November 28, 2018 via Google Books.

*We're all forced daily to make a choice, because the two sides are mutually exclusive.*

of real hungers squeezed between two structures, two sides, each challenging the other over common ground, yet yielding opposing outcomes—even though both promised to satisfy those hungers. And we're all forced daily to make a choice, because the two sides are mutually exclusive.

Looking at the hungers and the two opposing sides (the fruit of the Spirit versus the manifestations of the flesh), I wrestled with the fact that they both *seem* to promise satisfaction. What would make a person choose one over the other?

## MAKING A CHOICE

A French tightrope walker, Charles Blondin, traveled across the Atlantic Ocean and journeyed to Niagara Falls. He hoped to accomplish something that had never been done. He strung a 1,100-foot cable across the falls from the Canadian side to the United States side and prepared to walk across.

A large crowd watched as Blondin successfully crossed. But he wasn't finished. He grabbed a wheelbarrow, put a weight in it, and rolled it back, which impressed the crowd even more. Then Blondin turned to the crowd and asked, "How many of you believe I could put one of you in this wheelbarrow and roll you across?" Everybody said, "We believe!" But when he asked for volunteers, no one accepted his offer. Thousands believed; none of them trusted.

The incident has been used by many preachers to illustrate the difference between belief and trust. But Ken Boa makes an important point in his book *Rewriting Your Broken Story*[2]:

> It occurred to me, though, that there's something wrong with this illustration. Why would anyone get in the wheelbarrow? There would have to be a compelling reason.
>
> So try this: imagine that there was a thick forest behind the spectators and that suddenly caught fire. There was no way of escape. Now things get interesting, and suddenly all the rules change. Now there are only four options for the crowd:

---

2. Kenneth Boa, *Rewriting Your Broken Story: The Power of an Eternal Perspective* (Downers Grove, IL: IVP Books, 2016) Accessed March 4, 2018 via Google Books.

*Option number one: "I'm not here, and it's not hot." Deny your situation until you're burned to a crisp.*

*Option number two: take your chances by plunging into the raging water below.*

*Option number three: try to go across the tightrope yourself.*

*Option number four: get in the wheelbarrow!*

*Suddenly, the offer to get in Blondin's wheelbarrow looks very attractive. Furthermore, it's not a leap in the dark; it's a step into the light and perhaps your only real hope. He's already demonstrated that he could go to the other side and come back.*

We may not be able to precisely articulate the hungers we feel, but they're nonetheless undeniable. They're born within us and burn within us even when we ignore them or pretend they don't exist. Like physical hunger, the hunger will not go away until it's fed. The hunger drives us to a choice. The longer we refuse to choose, the more intense the pressure becomes. And eventually, we must choose the wheelbarrow or the flames.

*Like physical hunger, the hunger will not go away until it's fed.*

You're now ready to discover how these three lists can help you move toward satisfying your soul hungers. Keep in mind that only God and His Word hold the power for the renewal of the mind, body, and soul. In the flesh—meaning me without God—there actually dwells no good thing. So the flesh—minus God—is marginalized for any long-term effectiveness to satisfy any of your hungers, even when at first they seem gratified. Perhaps this truth is what prompted Solomon to write, "There is a way that appears to be right, but in the end it leads to death" (Proverbs 16:25 NIV).

*Only God and His Word hold the power for the renewal of the mind, body, and soul.*

In chapter 11 of this book you'll find a survey for evaluating your hungers. You can also visit www .hungertest.strikingly.com to take the same evaluation online. I urge you to take this evaluation soon. In fact, if you take it before you read the rest of this book, it will help you better understand the hunger(s) you're currently struggling with and trying to satisfy. The evaluation contains thirty-one questions, each having nine possible answers. As you follow the instructions for the evaluation, the hungers you're seeking to feed will become obvious. When you see your results, you may be tempted to dismiss them out of hand. Please don't. Remember, these are *your* answers, not my guesses.

Along with the evaluation I've provided an appendix (page 145) containing a thorough compilation of Scripture passages that parallel the hunger described in each chapter. Studying these Scriptures, along with some careful guidance I've included, will move you toward a more rewarding life of true fulfillment.

Now let's get started!

# CHAPTER 2

# THE HUNGER FOR INTIMACY

A growing body of evidence suggests isolation is hazardous to our health. Research presented at the 2017 American Psychological Association Annual Convention reported, "Loneliness and social isolation may represent a greater public health hazard than obesity. . . . Being connected to others socially is widely considered a fundamental human need."[3]

Simply stated, it's not good for you to let yourself be disconnected—to be a social hermit, if you will. The presentation also included results of studies that showed increased social interaction has a 50 percent reduced rate of early death.

Think about the very beginning of time—creation. The only "not good" spoken by God during the days was concerning man being alone and disconnected: "It is not good that man should be alone" (Genesis 2:18). Those words were spoken by an all-knowing, all-loving God. From the moment of creation, to be fully known yet fully loved—fully exposed yet fully accepted—was a universal yearning.

> *From the moment of creation, to be fully known yet fully loved—fully exposed yet fully accepted—was a universal yearning.*

---

3. American Psychological Association, "So Lonely I Could Die," American Psychological Association, August 5, 2017, https://www.apa.org/news/press/releases/2017/08/lonely-die.aspx.

It doesn't matter how much money or how much status you have; connection is an unavoidable, compelling human hunger. And Jesus understood. His prayer to the Father reflected this understanding. He prayed for His followers "that they may be one as We are" (John 17:11).

At some point in life, you'll have a deep, intrinsic, and sometimes evocative longing to be at one with something or someone. The longing, viscerally felt, is deeper than could ever be verbalized. It's an intrinsic longing because the necessity for connection is inherent in creation. And it's evocative because it hauntingly persists in our thoughts.

## ALONE IN A CROWDED ROOM

Norma Jean Mortensen's mother, Gladys Baker, was periodically committed to a mental institution, which meant Norma Jean spent much of her childhood in foster homes. In one of those foster homes, when she was eight years old, one of the boarders raped her, gave her a nickel, and told her not to tell anyone.

Norma Jean turned into a very pretty young girl, and people began to notice. But she always wished they would notice she was a person too—not just a body or a pretty face.

Arriving in Hollywood, Norma Jean took a new name—Marilyn Monroe. She was an overnight sensation, but she kept asking, "Did you also notice I'm a person?" No, they didn't notice.

So, on a Saturday night, at the age of thirty-six, when most beautiful women are in the presence of a handsome companion, Marilyn Monroe took her own life.

The next morning, Monroe's housekeeper found the telephone receiver dangling beside Monroe's lifeless body. In her article titled "What really killed Marilyn Monroe, love goddess who never found any love?" Clare Boothe Luce said she thought the dangling telephone was a symbol of Monroe's whole life, who died because she never got through to anyone who understood.

It was Albert Einstein who said about himself, "It is strange to be known so universally and yet to be so lonely." He echoes the words of generations.

Loneliness is keenly felt by so many in today's blogging, social media culture. These types of sites flourish because of our inner hunger to be connected. Online, we gather on "social" media where we develop networks of followers and circles of e-friends. Still, something isn't quite satisfying about all those virtual connections.

It's as natural for you to hunger for real personal connections as it is to hunger for oxygen. In a counseling session, a young college student told me about some advice he received on how to make new friends. He was told to go to gatherings where people his age were meeting. "Pastor," the young man told me, "I can be just as alone in a crowded room." He wasn't disconnected physically—yet he was still disconnected.

So where does the drive to be connected take you? What roads will it find? And will it satisfy the deep craving Norma Jean, Albert Einstein, and this young college student wanted so desperately? Most of all—will it satisfy you?

*It's as natural for you to hunger for real personal connections as it is to hunger for oxygen.*

One of the requirements for a class in the doctoral program at the seminary I attended included reading and critiquing the book *Connecting* by Dr. Larry Crabb. Examining his thoughts brought some pleasant surprises. One surprise in particular concerned those who aren't convinced that psychotherapy is the only way to health for those with psychological disorders.

What Dr. Crabb writes in his book resonates powerfully with the reader because he validates long-held skepticism of psychotherapeutic assumptions and techniques. Even better, he gives voice to skeptics who felt they had no standing to legitimately speak out because they're not trained psychologists. Their skepticism may have no academic basis, but these people's sense of mistrust is definite and deeply held.

Dr. Crabb communicates to the reader that after twenty-five-plus years as a psychologist, he reached a place that required him to shift the focus of his work. "Beneath what our culture calls psychological disorder," he writes, "is a soul crying out for what only community can provide."

He goes on to say that if these desperate souls do not find the nourishment of community, they'll die. He adds: "We must do something other than train professional experts to fix damaged psyches. Damaged psyches aren't the problem. The problem beneath our struggles is a disconnected soul."[4]

Reading Dr. Crabb's words just may take your thoughts back to the disconnected young man alone in a crowded room or to the screen name alone together with countless others seeking to be noticed on a crowded Internet.

---

4. Larry Crabb, *Connecting: Healing for Ourselves and Our Relationships* (Nashville: W Publishing Group, 1997). Accessed November 28, 2018 via Google Books.

# THE PRODUCT OF LONGING

An invitation came in the mail from my alma mater asking if I would participate in a weeklong special lecture modular. The college students were allowed to pick which subject interested them the most and attend those lectures. My assigned topic that day was abuse.

The lecture hall filled to overflowing. When I saw the faces of the students, I found myself in honest fear of handling such an intimate subject matter. Never having suffered the sort of abuse these students endured, could I offer content that truly related to them? A palpable loneliness could be sensed in the lecture hall—as though each person was playing a confidential game of solitaire of the heart.

Yet the room was crowded. The contrast was breathtaking.

The only noise inside the room, other than my voice from the lectern, was the occasional squeak of a chair or a self-conscious throat clearing.

At the end, the students left as quietly as they had sat.

I thought to myself, "Either the material was a bomb, or I nailed it. There could be no in between."

Later, their deep longing for connection, even intimacy, surfaced. The information given in the class began exposing the struggles within these young adults, and many individually reached out to me.

For the sake of privacy I won't mention any names. But I received more than a dozen letters in response to the material in my presentation that day. I still have them in a file in my desk drawer. If you could have been a fly on the wall in the classroom, you would have found simmering in their stories the battle of the temporal versus the eternal. It seemed they wanted to come across looking as though they had connections to others but didn't really want to pay the price demanded by genuine connection.

*God cannot heal deceit, He can only heal truth.*

When I made a particular statement in my lecture, "God cannot heal deceit, He can only heal truth," I could see it fully grabbed the attention of most in the room. Students later told me those words created a haunting echo in their minds. Too afraid that everyone around them had noticed their reaction, the room remained with a *morgue-like* silence.

"I do really want to be used of the Lord," said one student, Carla. "I only wish He could work through me without working in me!" Like the resonating heart cry of Norma Jean who only ever wanted to feel that someone loved her and cared about her, so many really never know how love is supposed to feel. And even through relationship after relationship, they still really don't.

It is easy to crawl into an emotional cocoon and become very hard to get to know . . . or to not allow yourself to get close to anyone because you can't deal with the failure of yet another relationship. Maybe that is why at times you don't even feel like your relationship with God is real.

At this point it is time to ask yourself the question, "Where do I go from here?" That's a question surely everyone eventually asks who seeks a healthy connection after years of pretense and superficial acquaintances. Upon finally growing weary of faking it, we wonder if there's any such thing as real connection. If so, where can we find it?

## SACCHARINE VERSUS SUGAR

The number-one hunger on my sticky-note list—intimacy—is being confronted by the initial imagery of the fruit of the Spirit and the manifestations of the flesh.

If you look back at the chart on page 15, you'll see the first production of the fruit of the Spirit is *love*. And not just any love, but *agape* love.

*Agape* is the English transliteration of a Greek word we see translated as *love* in our Bibles. Unlike English, which has only one word for love, the Greek language has four, and three of those are used in the New Testament. *Agape* identifies a love of the heart that's without sexual implications and also not rooted in family or affinity.

*Agape* is selfless, others-seeking love.

It's a love that's spiritual in nature.

A love that will never fail you.

Never forsake you.

Never abuse you.

Never use you.

*Agape* is love that represents an everlasting connection to the divine.

*Agape* is love that won't settle for mere perception. It demands reality; it demands truth!

This is the kind of connection the students were looking for yet were afraid would never happen.

> Agape *is love that represents an everlasting connection to the divine.*

Because connection is one of the things humans hunger for most, there are thousands of Norma Jeans in our world. *Agape* love would satisfy them all—if they would only make the choice to never allow imitators.

The problem is that on the opposite side of intimacy stands the counterfeit. It's the saccharine impersonating sugar, the temporal masquerading as the eternal.

*Adultery* and *fornication* masquerading as *agape!* And the hunger for connection pauses often in silence as it's positioned between the two—waiting for that choice, longing to be satisfied.

The counterfeits shout loudly. They scream, "I can satisfy your hunger!" They say they can connect with others, even generate intimacy—and indeed they can, for a season. To the isolated and the disconnected these imposters can feel so right. The flesh's cheap imitation is a seductive siren song, especially for people who desire connection so strongly they'll believe what they know to be a lie.

> The substitutes promise connection, but each delivers the aftertaste of bitter loneliness—and of shame, remorse, and regret.

The claim that fleeting physical closeness will genuinely satisfy a visceral longing for connection with others is indeed a lie and the inversion of truth. A satisfying physical intimacy is produced only by healthy, personal connection to another.

Still, many have chosen to try and satisfy the hunger for human connection with a superficial physical closeness instead of with *agape*. Yet only this first component of the fruit of the Spirit satisfies the hunger for connection with love, and its satisfaction is deeper and more permanent than adultery or fornication could ever presume.

*Agape* love—the kind of love God produces—is the real deal.

Tragically, on the other side stand the substitutes. They promise connection, but each delivers the aftertaste of bitter loneliness—and of shame, remorse, and regret.

## IT'S A DAILY CHOICE

In Deuteronomy 30, Moses speaks for the Lord when he tells God's people, "I call heaven and earth to witness against you today, that I have set before you life and death, the blessing and the curse. So choose life in order that you may live, you and your descendants" (v. 19 NASB).

*Choose life!* The choices we make in the significant moments of life help to shape us for good or bad. Choices also inform others about who we are and where we're going. Choices fuel us. Choices propel us to find the avenues through which we can redeem our experiences and purchase some wisdom.

If there was a way all your choices could become tangible and stacked up, they would be immediately recognizable because the choices you've made over the course of your life have sculpted the person you are today. Your choices look like you.

Carla defined her motives when she wrote, "I only wish He could work through me without working in me." Those words stick with me even to this day. And so many others manifest a similar attitude: living in the shadowlands of "if only." *If only I'd made better choices to quiet this hunger.*

God desires for everyone to experience true intimacy—to be truly connected. Everyone needs to know it's possible to choose such intimacy. And it is by *choice*, not by chance.

Every day, from the moment you waken, you face many choices—*Shall I get out of bed or roll over for more sleep? What do I wear? What will I have for breakfast?*

Choices, choices! But one choice makes all others pale in comparison.

Notice how Max Lucado framed it in his book *When God Whispers Your Name.* Writing about the fruit of the Spirit he says, "To these I commit my day. If I succeed, I will give thanks. If I fail, I will seek His grace." He goes on to explain how and why he daily chooses the fruit of the Spirit as opposed to the works of the flesh:

> *In a few moments the day will arrive. It will roar down the track with the rising of the sun. The stillness of the dawn will be exchanged for the noise of the day. The calm of solitude will be replaced by the pounding pace of the human race. The refuge of the early morning will*

*The choices we make in the significant moments of life help to shape us for good or bad. Choices also inform others about who we are and where we're going.*

*Your choices look like you.*

*be invaded by decisions to be made and deadlines to be met. For the next twelve hours I will be exposed to the day's demands. It is now that I must make a choice. Because of Calvary, I'm free to choose. And so I choose.*[5]

So the question is: To satisfy your hunger for connection, for intimacy—what will you choose today? Do you season your life with the eternal sweetness of love, or do you yield to the urge to choose adultery or fornication, so temporal and ultimately bitter?

Will you wake up in the morning and make a choice to descend into the works of the flesh? Or will you choose to ascend into the fruit of the Spirit?

It really is your choice!

ADULTERY/FORNICATION → INTIMACY ← LOVE

---

5. Max Lucado, *When God Whispers Your Name* (Nashville: Thomas Nelson, 1994) pp. 71 and 210.

# CHAPTER 3

# THE HUNGER FOR HAPPINESS

Around three hundred years before Christ, Aristotle wrote, "Happiness is the meaning and the purpose of life, the whole aim and end of human existence." While an argument might be made regarding whether happiness is as central to life's meaning as he asserts, the philosopher's observation certainly evidences how keenly and ubiquitously the hunger for happiness is felt among all people.

As Americans, we have a unique relationship to this hunger. Twenty centuries after Aristotle penned his lofty conclusion about happiness, an oppressed group of colonies in the New World rebelled against Great Britain by issuing a Declaration of Independence. Within this document, the founding fathers of the United States justified their revolt because of what they referred to as unalienable rights given to all people by the Creator. These rights are life, liberty, and the pursuit of happiness.

This pursuit of happiness is one of the most cherished rights we possess as citizens, and, like those who were driven to revolt when this right was stripped from them by the British Crown, generations of Americans have held this right as inviolable. This hunger of ours—the pursuit of happiness—has woven itself into the very fabric of our society.

And this hunger is so common, most people would say pursuing happiness is something we do instinctively. An important question is raised here, however: Though everyone may indeed be pursuing happiness, how many have actually captured it?

A 2017 Harris Poll cited in *Time* magazine gives something of an answer, revealing that only 33 percent of Americans say they are happy.[6] How remarkable that in a nation founded on the notion that all people have a right to pursue happiness, so few at any given time claim to have it.

That this hunger is so universally sensed yet so rarely satisfied compels us to ask a simple, crucial question: Why is this the case? The good news is there are definite answers to help us navigate this pursuit.

## QUESTIONS AND ANSWERS

The first thing we need to question is the nature of pursuing happiness. We must answer the question "How is happiness pursued?"

When we think of pursuit, we think of having some type of target or goal we're striving to catch or achieve. Once we know what we want, we usually pursue directly. "Carpe diem!" "Go for it!" and similar slogans all express the idea that once you identify a prize, you chase after it with vigor.

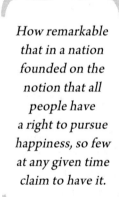

*How remarkable that in a nation founded on the notion that all people have a right to pursue happiness, so few at any given time claim to have it.*

Happiness, however, can't be pursued this way. In fact, happiness is a lot like magnets. Every magnet has both a north and a south pole. When you place like poles of two magnets near each other they will repel each other. When you first move your magnet toward the other, it moves, so you move your magnet faster whereupon the other moves faster out of the way.

No matter how quick you are, you simply cannot connect the magnets by moving one directly toward the other. This is happiness: no matter how insistently done, it can't be achieved by a direct pursuit.

Attempting to answer the question, "How is happiness pursued?" not only reveals that pursuing happiness directly can be equated with other desperately futile activities such as herding cats or spitting into the wind, but it also helps us understand that happiness is not something that can be pursued directly anyways. It is always the result of something else in our life.

---

6. Alexandra Sifferlin, "Here's How Happy Americans Are Right Now," *Times*, July 26, 2017, http://time.com/4871720/how-happy-are-americans/.

Happiness is actually a derivative of other things we experience, achieve, or choose. Think about it: No one sells happiness. There is no website or store or catalog where happiness can be purchased; no books exist on where to find happiness itself.

Instead, companies have learned to imply that happiness is the fruit of whatever it is they are attempting to sell to you. When you see any kind of advertising, the smiles, laughter, approval, and satisfaction are the happiness the product is implied to produce. In other words, the product is the means and happiness is the end.

When we say we are pursuing happiness, we are actually saying we are looking for things that will produce happiness. These might be things to explore or achieve; they might even be relationships.

*When we say we are pursuing happiness, we are actually saying we are looking for things that will produce happiness.*

The next question is about happiness itself. What do you think the 33 percent of Americans who say they are happy would say if you asked them, "Do you know for sure that you will still be happy next week? How about next month?"

We don't need a poll to know people who are happy today will likely say at some time in the near future that they are not as happy as they are right now. How many people who say they are happy today have discovered an everlasting fountain of happiness? Not a single one of them.

When the awful pain of a crushed and dejected spirit begins to suffocate us, choking us off from life, the pursuit of happiness becomes an all-consuming quest. It is a natural journey because, of course, the human hunger for happiness requests the merry heart rather than a crushed heart. Predictably the heart goes probing for whatever it believes will bring it happiness.

## YOU CAN HAVE
## WHAT YOU CHOOSE

John Wesley made interesting comments about this hunger for happiness in some of his personal notes. He wrote, "They shall have life that choose it: they that choose the favor of God, and communion with him, shall have what they choose. They that come short of life and happiness, must thank themselves only. They had had them, if they had chosen them, when they were put to their choice: but they die, because they will die."[7]

Interestingly, Wesley identifies the crushed heart then condenses its cause to a matter of choice. He is saying the meter of happiness is more likely to peg to the high side when we choose the favor and communion of God. If we awaken one day to the realization that the meter is at zero, and we find we are indeed not a happy person, we only have ourselves to blame.

That sounds harsh. Every day, we all make wrong choices. Does the right to choose really own such colossal power as Wesley says? Yes, I believe it does. In Deuteronomy 30:19 Moses told the people under his leadership that he called heaven and earth that day to witness against them, that he set in front of them life and death, blessings and cursings. "Choose life!" he cries. According to this passage, the power that choosing holds in its grip extends even to life, death, blessings, and cursings.

The well-respected commentator Matthew Henry seems to agree. Look at the contrasting conditions he confronts in letting us know from where he believes happiness comes.

> What could be said more moving, and more likely to make deep and lasting impressions? Every man wishes to obtain life and good, and to escape death and evil; he desires happiness, and dreads misery. So great is the compassion of the Lord, that he has favored men, by his word, with such a knowledge of good and evil as will make them forever happy, if it be not their own fault. Let us hear the sum of the whole matter. If they and theirs would love God, and serve him, they should live and be happy. If they or theirs should turn from God, desert his service . . . that would certainly be their ruin.[8]

## PURSUING HAPPINESS

What is the nature of happiness? Simply stated, it isn't a state we can live in; it is more like moments we seek, and these moments can't be captured and held forever. Happiness is inherently fickle and fleeting; its potency diminishes as each day passes.

---

7. "Deuteronomy 30 Bible Commentary," John Wesley's Explanatory Notes, Christianity.com, accessed November 14, 2018, http://www.christianity.com/bible/commentary.php?com=wes&b=5&c=30.

8. "Deuteronomy 30," Matthew Henry Commentary on the Whole Bible (Concise), biblestudy tools.com, accessed November 14, 2018, https://www.biblestudytools.com/commentaries/matthew-henry -concise/deuteronomy/30.html.

The reason happiness must be sought lies in the fact it can't be experienced simply because of who we are. David Myers, author of *The Pursuit of Happiness*, released an article in *Psychology Today* that discussed his findings regarding happiness:

> *If I wanted to predict whether you feel happy and find life satisfying, there are some things that, surprisingly, it would not help me to know. For example: Tell me your age, and you've given me no clue. . . . Tell me your sex, and you've given me no clue. . . . Tell me your race, and you've given me no clue. . . . Tell me your income, and—assuming you can afford life's necessities—I'm still in the dark as to whether you're a happy person.*[9]

In other words, happiness is not a by-product of where we're from, how old or what gender we are, or how much money we make—all things everyone can easily answer. Happiness is something that lies outside the sphere of the people we are or will become.

Because of this, happiness must also be continually renewed or recaptured, but sometimes the means by which we experienced it before aren't as effective in seizing it the next time.

*Happiness is something that lies outside the sphere of the people we are or will become.*

For example, watch a child at Christmas. The happiness found around a Christmas tree bulging with gifts is without comparison. In the midst of mountains and canyons of discarded wrapping paper, kids revel in the gifts they've hoped for and anticipated since Thanksgiving.

Ask most any parent, and they'll tell you the celebration over these gifts is typically gone by New Year. By then, the wonder and newness of the gifts are gone, and oftentimes, kids rarely show an interest in playing with many of those toys ever again.

What's more, you can't reproduce the happiness experienced on the morning of December 25 by wrapping those same presents and presenting them to the same children on the morning of, say, January 4. The happiness those toys

---

9. David Meyers, "Pursuing Happiness," *Psychology Today*, last reviewed June 9, 2016, https://www.psychologytoday.com/us/articles/199307/pursuing-happiness.

generated at Christmas is gone. It can't be had again, even by recreating the exact same situation.

The same can be said about happiness in general and the difficulty we have in sustaining it. Because it's not generated by anything constant or inherent about us, we must seek it through means outside of us. Because happiness is fleeting, the same means will probably not result in the same success more than a few times.

Which brings us to the problem of satisfying the hunger for happiness: it's usually a moving target.

## CAN HAPPINESS BE PURSUED?

There is a reason why so many common expressions have arisen in culture that equate pursuing happiness with such desperate activities like herding cats, spitting into the wind, or grabbing hold of lightning. Because of its elusive nature, pursuing happiness is as futile an exercise as any of these. The pursuit itself usually turns out to be an unhappy experience because of the nature of the word. Here are a few other words that come from the same root as our word *happy*. Recognizing the relationship of these words to happiness should help us realize that happiness at best is an elusive commodity.

*Because happiness is fleeting, the same means will probably not result in the same success more than a few times.*

Happenstance.

Haphazard.

Hapless.

Happenchance.

Do you see the common thread here? The word *happy* came into our vocabulary around 1205 from an Old Norse word *happ*, meaning luck or chance, and from a Proto Germanic word, *khapan*, meaning good fortune. So if we ever reach a state of happiness, by sheer definition, it is merely coincidental.

*God says He gives us a happiness that cannot be affected by outward circumstance.*

So we don't really pursue happiness, do we? We pursue events and circumstances we hope contain some form of happiness to our liking. But we're still not sure if we'll find the happiness we're looking for, are we? It's like a grab bag that promises to contain a surprise, but you never really know what is going to be in the bag. Nonetheless, the possibility of a happy surprise coming out of the bag makes the pursuit worthy to us.

For me, the solution for the happiness pursuit is stuck on the wall of my office. We hunger for happiness, but God says He gives us a happiness that cannot be affected by outward circumstance. It does not come to us by chance. In fact, what God provides isn't happiness at all. It's more than that!

*It is joy!*

I have heard of a few people attempting to muster a convincing argument that joy can be pursued. But when I hear *pursuit* and *joy* in the same sentence, it doesn't compute. I think back to what the psalmist wrote when he said, "Joy *comes* with the morning" (Psalm 30:5 ESV, emphasis added).

"Joy *comes*," he writes.

Joy, if you just "be still and know that [He is] God" (Psalm 46:10), is like the beautiful butterfly that will come and sit on your shoulder.

Joy is God-given through the fruit of the Spirit, not manufactured through works of the flesh. "As the deer pants for the water brooks, so my soul pants for You, O God" (Psalm 42:1 NASB). That is how joy appears! It comes when our soul pants for God!

To get *happiness* we pursue gratifying circumstances. To get *joy*, we pursue God.

*Joy is God-given through the fruit of the Spirit, not manufactured through works of the flesh.*

*To get happiness we pursue gratifying circumstances. To get joy, we pursue God.*

His Holy Spirit will produce within us a joy that is unspeakable and full of glory: a delight that cannot be purchased or gained by a hungry pursuit of exhilarating events.

C. S. Lewis, in his book *The Weight of Glory*, sums it up: "Our Lord finds our desires not too strong, but too weak. We are half-hearted creatures, fooling about with drink and sex and ambition when infinite joy is offered us, like an ignorant child who wants to go on making mud pies in the slum because he cannot imagine what is meant by the offer of a holiday at the sea. We are far too easily pleased."[10]

---

10. C. S. Lewis, "The Weight of Glory," in *The Weight of Glory and Other Addresses*, ed. Walter Hooper (New York: Simon & Schuster, 1996), 25–26.

## A Vapor Trail

Have you ever seen one of those giant commercial jets streaking across the sky on a clear day? You probably noticed it first by its vapor trail. Although the white trail looms even larger than the plane and helps locate it in the ubiquitous blue, it holds no power. It doesn't propel the jet forward; it only serves to show the path of the forward movement of the plane. The trail can even give an idea, by its short history, of the direction the plane is heading and is likely to continue to go. But no pilot would ever tell you that there is influence in the vapor. It commands no authority.

The vapor trail is much like the wake a boat leaves as it negotiates the waterways. The sailor can look at the wake and tell where he has been, but a continuous looking backward at the wake won't tell him where he is headed. On the contrary, looking backward is a recipe for certain danger in forward movement. Similarly, if we are to *pursue* happiness, it means a forward movement rather than a reverse look.

This is sadly evident about far graver issues in life as well. Aging marriages can't find happiness again by staging another wedding; the same bonus received with gladness from work this year will eventually be despised if left unchanged each successive year; as children grow, we can't usher happiness into their life with simple trips to get ice cream.

There is a caveat in the investment world cautioning potential investors that past performance does not guarantee future success. No truer statement could be crafted concerning happiness; the past is not a place to find happiness. Still, many pursue it by consulting past performances of various means wherein they previously found happiness. In so doing, many live stroking these memories, trying to recreate happiness as intensely and futilely as the explorer Ponce De León ran after the fountain of youth!

The problem of attempting to satisfy the hunger for happiness is it can't be had by merely repeating the actions and circumstances of past happiness. New and different means must be sought. When people speak of "pursuit of happiness," they are talking about the means they employ they hope will produce happiness.

This is the heart of happiness as revealed in Galatians 5.

If you find a familiar refrain in this book, hopefully it is that the flesh offers shortcuts to satisfy the hungers we sense. Shortcuts offer quicker ways to arrive at a certain destination, but they usually present risks for the convenience.

> *The flesh offers shortcuts to satisfy the hungers we sense.*

The flesh is a master of marketing the advantages of the quick and easy while obscuring the many risks involved. While conventional wisdom asserts there's no shortcut to happiness, the flesh has the audacity to hold out two for everyone's consideration: uncleanness and lewdness. If we are going to refuse shortcuts in our pursuit of happiness, we must understand what these two ugly words represent in the choices we all face daily.

## THERE IS A CHOICE

We have a choice as to which side we find ourselves. Standing beside the hunger for happiness are a couple of substitute hucksters—uncleanness and lewdness—waving to us to come aside so they might peddle their own brand of happiness. These are two of the works of the flesh Satan offers as substitutes for joy. Uncleanness is anything not pure or is defiled, something that turns the heart away from righteousness. Jesus taught there is no ceremonial uncleanness, only moral and spiritual uncleanness. It is not what goes into a person's mouth that defiles them but what proceeds out of their heart. If you want a name attached to the unclean, try *evil thoughts, hatred, adultery, murder,* and so forth— words that are not strangers to our ears and need no definition. It is the unclean things of Galatians 5 that pollute the man.

*The flesh is a master of marketing the advantages of the quick and easy while obscuring the many risks involved.*

Then there is lewdness, or what some translations call licentiousness, which is an excessive indulgence of liberty, a lacking of moral restraints, especially the disregarding of sexual boundaries, lacking decorum, or immoral acts. This happens when our liberty is allowed to become an authorization for anything that feels good in the moment.

There is perhaps no better illustration of the two than the hunger for happiness that goes on during a college road trip to the beach every spring break. Advertisers, advocates, and aficionados of a Florida spring break flood social media. The evening news will offer video confirmation of the "fun" to be had. Clothes shedding without shame, societal decorum being violated, and reckless, gratuitous physical engagements of every sort become the norm for the entire week. Calling this kind of behavior "happiness" is like calling a manure patty a pecan pie. It is cheap thrills being tossed about as joyful occasions, something worthy of their attention. The participants are like giddy teenagers looking for a car to take on some sort of a joyride. It usually ends with damaged possessions, if not in tragedy.

Consider Esteban. Esteban sat in my office a broken individual. He had been there many times before. His usual defiant, superior self wasn't present this time, and I was wondering where that part of him went. His story is epic. You name it, and he has tried it. His experience is much like many American college students today who go to university actually expecting to learn the fine art of falling into uncleanness and lewdness in lieu of a classic education. Esteban made a stark turn from the Christian upbringing experienced in his home. The words, "I told you so," leapt to the tip of my tongue, but my tightly shut teeth and lips wouldn't let them out. The hucksters of manufactured happiness were just too attractive for him to resist. He found himself headed to prison, and on this day, strangely, he wanted me to vouch for him as a character witness.

"You do have a choice," I said to Esteban, "to ascend into joy—the true source of happiness—or to descend where you have been for a while now, into the squalor of cheap thrills that the works of the flesh offer."

It is true that when one pursues the deceptive works of the flesh, they will experience a fleeting kind of happiness better described as a thrill—a cheap, manufactured, human thrill. It is more like a buzz that brings with it the wages of death earned in the sweaty fleshly pursuit of happiness.

Esteban has tasted and swallowed the saccharine. The agony on his face was a witness to the bitterness of its pursuit. But another journey began . . . a different pursuit. The pursuit of God to encounter real happiness called joy!

## THE OFFER OF JOY

Speaking to His closest friends, Jesus said, "These things I have spoken to you, that My joy may remain in you, and that your joy may be full" (John 15:11).

My joy . . . your joy.

He connected the two. Joy is the legacy Jesus was leaving with them. He wanted it to remain in them and with them. A few sentences before this remark, Jesus explained they could experience that joy when there is a vital connection, a union, with Him. He illustrated it with the comparison of a vine and a branch. The branch slumps from the vine into the surrounding dirt looking for a happy place to put down roots. God, the vinedresser, has to come along and lift it up. If we humanized the branch we could say the branch will forget the vine and attempt to put down roots wherever it can find happiness. Likely it will find it in shallow soil . . . in places it should not be taking root.

Writing in his book *The Myth of Happiness* of his experience with the feuding extremes of joy and happiness, author Rich Wagner said:

> *Happiness is all about the here and now. Biblical joy is rooted in eternity . . . "There is no happiness; there are only moments of happiness," says an Old Spanish proverb. Joy, on the other hand, combines both: a constant presence of God inside me sprinkled with moments of genuine delight.*
>
> *Time is the archenemy of happiness, but it is joy's best friend. By its nature, happiness is impatient. Joy, on the other hand, can afford to wait. It knows it has eternity to enjoy. Happiness depends on circumstances, but joy is independent of anything that happens to me. . . .*
>
> *Pain kills happiness, but joy soothes pain. Not surprisingly, happiness demands that I flee pain at all cost. Joy, by contrast, is open to the suffering that results from obeying Jesus Christ.*[11]

I can't help but believe there may be people who, like Esteban, have been happiness seekers for a long time. Who have been so hungry for happiness they have tasted everything offered them and still have an empty belly. And there may be those who perhaps have never considered that a connection with God could produce a fulfilling joy within . . . a joy so full they could cease searching for thrills and enjoy the true happiness the fruit of the Spirit gives. I am hoping those who once were connected to that joy, but for whatever reason have been seduced by the purveyors of the works of the flesh, will do a 180 and head back to the groves where the sweet fruit grows. Because as psychologist Larry Crabb writes, "Many of us place top priority not on becoming Christlike in the middle of our problems but on finding happiness. . . . I must firmly and consciously by an act of my will reject the goal of becoming happy and adopt the goal of becoming more like the Lord. The result will be happiness for me as I learn to dwell at God's right hand in fellowship in Christ."[12]

## UNCLEANNESS/LICENTIOUSNESS → HAPPINESS ← JOY

---

11. Rich Wagner, *The Myth of Happiness: Discovering a Joy You Never Thought Possible* (Grand Rapids: Zondervan, 2007), 25.

12. Larry Crabb, *Effective Biblical Counseling: A Model for Helping Caring Christians Become Capable Counselors* (Grand Rapids: Zondervan, 2013). Accessed November 28, 2018, via Google Books.

# CHAPTER 4

# THE HUNGER FOR CONTENTMENT

A while back I was working through some feelings and found myself not satisfied with the direction of my personal thought processes. So I asked my author friend Steve Van Winkle to think through *contentment* versus *discontentment* and correspond with me. I wanted to find out what brings a previously contented person so close to the edge of disappointment that they consider walking away frustrated and discontented. After writing back and forth about the subjects, we came to some interesting conclusions, but one is particularly useful when considering this hunger for contentment: we noticed many people have had experiences in their lives—both positive and negative—that are now rotting without redemption.

All that we have seen, learned, and done from these experiences should not only be able to help us navigate a course in life but also bless others who are able to exchange them for wisdom in their own lives. Our experiences have the potential to be treasures of wisdom for the people we love.

*Many people have had experiences in their lives—both positive and negative—that are now rotting without redemption.*

## Portraits in Contentment

Try to find statistics about contentment on the Internet; they're hard to uncover. Usually, those numbers are buried somewhere in polls and studies on "happiness," as though being content is a function of being happy.

If you look around, you'll discover many unhappy people who are content. As we said in chapter 3, happiness is not a state we can live in; it's a moving target. Contentment, on the other hand, is pervasive when present in life.

*Contentment is more about us than about our circumstances.*

You can be happy for a time, happy with something, happy about an achievement, happy about myriad things—most of them temporary. But contentment is more about us than about our circumstances; indeed, it is most starkly seen when what we are experiencing seems that it would amount to anything but contentedness.

Discontentment is responsible for an impressive list of lamentable choices and decisions from people who would typically give most anything to have another chance to make different ones. Granted, sometimes discontentment is the impetus to accepting challenges and creating a better life, but the most common type of discontentment is usually the kind that gnaws at people to trade in current circumstances for unrealized better ones.

*When motivated purely by discontent, what people end up with is rarely what they hoped to find.*

When motivated purely by discontent, what people end up with is rarely what they hoped to find.

What people hunger for is contentment that transcends the circumstances around them; they search for satisfaction in ultimate things so the annoyances of incidental and passing ones don't dictate their emotions. There is a good example of this kind of lifestyle in the Bible.

The disciples have to be the most contented collection of people ever to walk the earth. From the moment they met Jesus their lives were marked by sacrifice and active resistance: some of these men had friends betray them while others sacrificed lucrative careers; they spent their adult lives dependent on the generosity of others for their sustenance; they were beaten by strangers and abandoned by family; and some spent significant time incarcerated.

Still, other than Judas, none ever quit. No disciple ever decided to find a better job or try to change their message so more people would like them. None broke off from the others to start something better of their own, and no one lamented the amount of perceived success they were unable to achieve.

These men epitomized contentment. Their circumstances shifted and shaded, mostly from bad to worse, but they always moved forward without falling to chronic regret over what they had left behind or what seemed always out of reach.

If they had the contentment so many hunger after, we would be wise to try and discover how, where, and when they managed to graft contentment into their lives. I believe it all goes back to John 14.

Discontentment came naturally under the heavy boot of Roman persecution, and perhaps that was what dislodged these men from their lives to the point that leaving everything to follow this homeless Jesus seemed a step up. And then, three years later, in this upper room, Jesus told them He was leaving; moreover, they could not go with Him.

Not that day.

Not the next.

The emotion in the room was palpable, being equal parts confusion, clamoring, and chaos. The varied conversations give evidence of it.

I can almost hear the disciples' thoughts in my mind. *Three years ago each of us hooked our wagon to His star, and now He's standing in front of us telling us not only He's leaving but also we can't come along?*

After a verbal exchange challenging their raw emotions, Jesus settled everything with these assurances: "Peace I leave with you, My peace I give to you; not as the world gives do I give to you. Let not your heart be troubled, neither let it be afraid" (v. 27).

Jesus summed up what He had in mind for these men by leaving them with three powerful heartening contemplations.

"I want you peaceful!" *My peace I give to you.* Not the absence of conflict but an underlying contentment that generates an unspeakable peace.

"I want you untroubled!" *Let not your heart be troubled.*

"I want you unafraid!" *Neither let it be afraid.*

Condensing His remarks into one word, He is leaving them with . . . *peace.*

What more could anyone want? Jesus knew the problem these men would soon face was not a problem of circumstance but a problem of the heart. If He had seen the coming circumstances as the problem, perhaps He would have promised them security or told them the cause was bigger than the resistance.

He didn't. He promised peace. Peace is what people sense within themselves regardless of the circumstances buzzing about them. Jesus could not promise the disciples that their lives were going to be celebrated and carefree; He'd be lying to them if so. What He could promise, however, was that while they were enduring trials, want, and isolation, they would know inexplicable peace.

In the years that followed, people would naturally wonder why none of these men made "adjustments" so their lives wouldn't be such a continual uphill struggle. But what wasn't visible from the outside, however, was the peace within these disciples of Jesus. This peace leaves no room for discontent. What Christ left with His disciples is the key to satisfying our innate hunger for contentment.

*Peace is what people sense within themselves regardless of the circumstances buzzing about them.*

In the Upper Room, the disciples were troubled, and Jesus knew that having a troubled state of mind freezes out contentment from any life. While it is possible to sense overall contentment in the midst of troubling situations, when people feel troubled about their life in general or in a variety of key areas, discontentment soon seeps in and becomes not only the operating principle of their lives but an all-consuming obsession.

Jesus knew that a troubled life would lead to discontentment, and a discontented group of disciples would be at best highly ineffective! Consequently, nothing Jesus could give them would prepare them more than this treasure of peace.

In the description of Anne Woodcock's book, *Contentment: Healing the Hunger of Our Hearts*, it says, "The Bible shows that discontent is the symptom of a lethal disease that will kill us if we do not find a cure. It was discontent that first led humans into rebellion against God, with the catastrophic consequences that have followed from that decision. . . . Discontent is a problem of our hearts not our circumstances."[13]

Peace is what the Lord left for His disciples to foster contentment in a lifestyle that would demand much sacrifice and promise virtually no earthly enrichment. If the testimony of their lives is any indication, peace was certainly the cornerstone to lives of contentment.

---

13. Anne Woodcock, *Contentment: Healing the Hunger of Our Hearts* (Epsom, Surrey: The Good Book Company, 2008).

When the hunger for contentment in a world designed to breed its opposite gnaws most deeply, this same peace Jesus promised His disciples in the Upper Room remains the only genuine means for fully satisfying it. This is why John 14 isn't the last place we read about disciples and peace.

Our list in Galatians holds it out for every successive generation of disciples to lay hold of so they can live contented in a turbulent world. Though our situations are different from the original disciples', how can we appropriate the peace that ushers us into contentment?

## THE PEACE PROCESS

Jesus mentions many things in this discourse in John 14, all of them vital. His final exhortation contains a small nugget about Himself that is intriguing but easily overlooked because at first glance it doesn't appear significant.

In verse 30, Christ remarks that the "ruler of this world"—Satan—is coming for Him; this is Jesus' declaration that the climax of the ageless plan of redemption is now underway, and He will be apprehended and taken to be crucified. Almost off-handedly, He mentions that this ruler "has nothing in Me."

In our terms, the phrase means, "He's got nothing on me." Jesus says there is nothing within Him the enemy can exploit for evil purposes. As the unspeakable cruelty of the Cross loomed before Him, Jesus was focused on accomplishing God's plan and was free from the turmoil of being troubled like His disciples.

This surprises no one. After all, who would expect Jesus to have anything the devil could use for his purposes? It bears knowing that, being the Second Person of the Trinity, Christ is what theologians call "very God," meaning completely God; however, at the Incarnation, Christ was also "very man." Jesus is the 200-percent person, if you will.

The writer of Hebrews described Christ as being tempted in every way we could have been yet was without sin. So it should be remembered that when Jesus says the devil had nothing on Him, this is not some unattainable privilege or power of deity. It lays out at least a goal we must seek to sense the kind of peace that satisfies our hunger for contentment.

An essential part of the peace process is understanding what prevents us from acquiring peace. When nations or disputing parties come to the table they hope for reconciliation. One of the first things that must be covered is what is currently happening that threatens future peace.

So it is for us; we must be aware of things within us that mark our lives and prevent peace from taking root. This process includes eliminating the things the enemy could use to disrupt any potential peace in the future.

While compiling a one-size-fits-all list is not practical because the types of issues range from universal to extremely personal, we can examine a common item; in doing so, we can also foster an awareness of others that could mean trouble to the peace process. To do so, we need to go back to the key point that began this chapter.

## ROTTING WITHOUT REDEMPTION

My friend Steve is right. People have experiences that are only that . . . experiences. As people age, there is a longing to know their life has meaning, that they have mattered. In the absence of meaning, the enemy will exploit this longing because even a well-lived life with unredeemed experiences brings trouble eventually.

What does "unredeemed experiences" mean? Simply that what we've gone through (good and bad), what we've learned (formally and informally), and even the people we've known long to be exchanged for wisdom in the lives of others. If we don't redeem them through investment and interest in those who are coming behind us, we become troubled, seeing our life as having only amounted to a few stories hanging uselessly from hooks on which we display our past dreams, past regrets, and even past relationships.

We can't escape sensing that these experiences should be worth something other than just rotting, pesky memories. They should become memorable life lessons, and we should be able to squeeze some wisdom from them to pass down to our children, friends, and family in Christ in hopes they might profit from our mistakes or benefit from our accomplishments. In the absence of this greater worth, we give the enemy of peace something with which he can stir the pot of discontent in our life.

This truth was never as clear to me as it was when I received an unexpected note from a member of my church informing me he was going into the hospital the next day for open-heart surgery.

In the note he explained that he'd had a premonition he would not make it through the surgery, and he wanted me to know how much my teaching had meant to him and how he experienced growth under my leadership. While I appreciated the compliment, my immediate concern was for his life and his family. So I got up early the next morning and went to his hospital prep room to pray with him.

Once there, he expressed how his experiences (and they were myriad) were laying strewn like body bags in the wake of his past. He had kept them to himself

THE HUNGER FOR CONTENTMENT

and had shared them with neither his sons nor his wife. Some of these experiences embarrassed him; some made him happy; but all were just hanging there decaying, rotting without redemption.

After we talked and prayed, he declared before he went into surgery that if God brought him through, he would correct this path and share the wisdom and life lessons of his past with those he loved. The surgery was indeed successful!

After, he rarely missed church and his knowledge of Scripture seemed to grow with each day. He was true to his word and shared his experiences freely and, if you had time to listen, life lessons came with each one. What was truly remarkable was the wave of contentment that washed over his life from a simple determination to redeem his life experiences birthed from the turmoil of facing the prospect of never again having the chance.

While my friend survived that surgery, four years later he slumped over on his porch dead; he was finally released from his failing body to be at home with Christ. At his funeral, I heard his boys eulogize their father with the same stories and lessons he pledged to share with them four years earlier.

*Key to the peace process is emptying ourselves of anything the enemy of peace can use to trouble us.*

My friend was given a new opportunity to invest the events of his life, and he seized it. The last four years of investing his life in those he knew and loved moved his experiences from dead stories the enemy could have used to trouble him with regret, anger, and self-pity to a source of great peace and contentment.

Key to the peace process is emptying ourselves of anything the enemy of peace can use to trouble us. This might be anything from a regret over not achieving a simple goal to regret over a lifetime's worth of experiences rotting unredeemed in the hallway of our memories. Whatever it might be, it should be identified, dealt with, and jettisoned as quickly as possible because every moment we delay is another day driven by discontentment.

## FILLING THE VOID

There's an interesting habit of Scripture many never understand. When the Bible exhorts us to put something off, it always tells us to put something in place of it. Contrary to what many accuse it of, the Bible is not a list of don'ts; it never prescribed a *don't* where it does not also hold up a *do*.

So it is with the peace process. Certainly, there are things we must deal with and remove if we are to finally attain the peace we seek, but there are things we must also do if we are to capture it.

To know God's peace consistently, which He assures us passes all understanding and brings with it true contentment, we must pursue it through a relationship with His Son, Jesus. This term, *relationship*, is often open to a variety of understandings, but at its core, is the notion of grateful obedience.

> *This term, relationship, is often open to a variety of understandings, but at its core, is the notion of grateful obedience.*

God once indicted Israel for serving Him with their lips but having a heart that was "far from" Him (Isaiah 29:13). We aren't talking about that kind of rote, timid, even fearful obedience; the relationship-building obedience necessary for peace flows from a deep gratitude for our salvation and the privilege of knowing God.

Jesus Himself set the parameters for this relationship when He told His disciples they were His friends if they were completely obedient to His will (John 15:14). This is our standard as well; the things we know to do as His disciples must be found in our lives. Disobedience affects our relationship with Him, not our "sonship," as the prodigal son discovered. But the peace that passes all understanding is available only through grateful obedience.

## ACCEPT NO SUBSTITUTE

While Paul's list in Galatians offers us the pathway to contentment through peace, he is also careful to warn us that flesh offers its own avenue to what many discover too late is an empty promise. The world calls it religion and seeks to offer it as a forgery; it's typically served up as a deceptively good-feeling relationship with artificial gods of their own imagination.

> *They were His friends if they were completely obedient to His will (John 15:14).*

In truth, those in this counterfeit religion worship the creature rather than the Creator. The flesh and the world hold out for exaltation a god of the people, by the people, and for the people. But this god of theirs has no expectation of us and is certainly not the God of the Bible.

Ultimately, this type of saccharine religion is little more than the idolatry Paul puts a label to in Galatians. At times, we can be tempted to sprinkle the saccharine of idolatry over our discontented mind to sweeten life, exchanging a dynamic love and peace for a pseudo relationship with imposters.

Idolatry comes in many forms other than religion. It might be a person we idolize; it could be a certain status or even freedom and security. Literally nothing is out of idolatry's reach. And the flesh will certainly offer it up as a satisfying alternative to the peace offered by the only true God. In the end, however, imbibing synthetically sequenced religion hoping to find lasting peace may work temporarily, but in the end it will only multiply our discontent.

From the moment I met Alan, I knew there was something special about him. He was an artist of the best kind. His poetry was off-the-charts expressive. He was one of those young men who only comes along once in a great while. He and I connected immediately. His work was worthy of being published, so I made sure it was. Thousands of people across America, as well as overseas, were saying his lines and believing them deeply. When reading his poetry, there was no doubt of his deep relationship with his God, his shepherd, his King, his Savior.

Unfortunately, time passes faster than we wish in our relationships, leaving unwanted gaps of time in between conversations. My relationship with Alan was no exception. One day a few months ago, after the passing of thirty-five unnoticed years, I received an email from Alan.

After all these years, we finally reconnected.

However, it wasn't long into our renewed friendship when Alan dropped an IED in my world. Not an *improvised explosive device* but an *immediate explosion of discontentment.* He told me how he came to be an atheist. That he now believes God is an imaginary being and creation is a myth. He has found a new enlightenment, and it is rooted not in God but in man and intellect. He now lives by the golden rule, which he believes preceded Jesus, and when the end comes, well . . . the end comes. He says it with frightening conviction and of course with artistry.

In the course of our email exchanges lately, his discontentment with past truths not lived out by others began to surface. The values he thought would work for him back when we first met somehow didn't work any longer. He looked for an answer on the wrong side of contentment. I found him steeped in seemingly inextricable idolatry. In his eyes, man and intellect is greater than an illusory God.

But the peace Alan is looking for to satisfy the hunger for contentment is located where he refuses to search . . . the fruit of the Spirit.

## THE SHORTCUTS OF
## TODAY'S SORCERY

Paul identifies in Galatians a second substitute held out by the flesh. The hunger for contentment is so acute people often resort to an immediate fix of peace found in what Paul labeled "sorcery."

Sorcery seems too medieval to be relevant to anyone today, but in Scripture the word *sorcery* is from the Greek word *pharmakeia*, from where we get the word *pharmacy*. While it's a mistake to label pharmacies or pharmacology as sorcery, the parallel is important because both refer to the use of drugs.

Pharmacology today offers drugs for health, while sorcery in Paul's day ranged from illicit drugs to actual contact with spirits. In my study of biblical sorcery, I am convinced it is nothing more than the search for insight or peace through mind-altering substances or peeks into the past or future by contacting departed souls.

And, as outrageous as it might seem, we have parallels to it today. Just like the Lord offers His peace to every successive generation of disciples, so the flesh offers its own version by holding out its substitutes to every successive generation.

This generation is no exception.

You can find it in the frightening proliferation of illicit drugs and drug use. These offer instant gratification for escaping whatever plagues people; they are quick jolts of peace and contentment for people who have neither.

Problem is, drugs never actually deal with what is preventing peace in someone, and the users come down from their highs to the same discontent and turmoil from which they sought escape only hours previously. Too often, the solution to this disappointment is more substance abuse, perhaps even more powerful than the previous substance, which soon spins into addiction. The sad result being only multiplied turmoil as those who were searching for a little contentment have instead exponentially increased its opposite.

Along with illicit drugs, prescription psychotropic drugs have also become a great concern in our society. There is no disputing that these are godsends for people truly needing chemical help to have clarity of thought and mind. Along with this, however, is a national plague of over-prescribing such pills to people whose problem isn't so much chemical as it is emotional and spiritual.

There is indeed a medical contentment that can be found through these compounds when prescribed correctly, but for people who are not in true need of them, these drugs can mask the patient's actual need in life—God's peace.

God holds out His offer of peace, but too many people opt for what seems the quick and easy way to satisfy their contentment hunger only to find that it gets further away with each sunrise.

The other side of sorcery is found today in people looking for peace from those claiming to be able to tell the future or contacting the "other side." The greatest source of troubling emotions and concerns is the future; people fret over what is coming or what might happen to them or their loved ones.

In response the flesh holds out an option that circumvents trusting the Lord and pursuing a relationship with Him. The world deceives people into believing they can know the future now. Of course, the future is only for the Lord to know, and the peace derived from any communication with one who practices sorcery is short-lived, because there is always an unknown future looming.

The peace offered by God is so much better than the substitutes held out by the flesh. God, as opposed to idols, is living and knows our needs and promises to meet them freely and fully; God has never been sued for breach of contract. He also inhabits tomorrow, and unlike drugs or fortune-tellers of all kinds, He can direct us into a better future by changing us or, if necessary, changing tomorrow.

What healthier human desire is there other than to be content—to live life free from the nagging pull to own what everybody else has, plus a little more, to be satisfied with how God created us individually, so as not to covet others' gifts and talents? How comforting it would be to be satisfied and not feel the pull to look into the flesh's bag of tricks and pull out a counterfeit.

God wants you to be peaceful, untroubled, and unafraid. You have the choice to descend into the deep pit sucking you down into the dark vortex of idolatry and sorcery; many do.

Or you can choose today to ascend into the peace of God where real contentment has its roots!

## IDOLATRY/SORCERY → CONTENTMENT ← PEACE

# CHAPTER 5

# THE HUNGER
# FOR JUSTICE

W ho knew there were so many children in this family?

If everybody lined up against the wall in alphabetical order to shout their first names for the Justice family photo, you'd hear: "Criminal," "Distributive," "Environmental," "Juvenile," "Procedural," "Reparative," "Restorative," "Retributive," "Social." Indeed, they all have their importance, and each is fascinating in its own way. But when they all shout out their names as loudly as they can in order to be heard over the screams of their siblings, they create a cacophony of commotion around the word *justice* that is mostly unnecessary.

Justice by any other name is still defined as justice. Asking, "Which justice do you want today?" is like asking, "Which slice of the pie would you like to have today?" A slice from the left side tastes the same as a slice from the right side. Move the pie tin around to slice the apple pie at any place and you still have . . . apple pie. Slice it thin or slice it fat, it doesn't matter. The same goes for our hunger for justice. Justice by any other name is still justice.

What I want to do is introduce you to the father of all these justices. Mr. Justice . . . God! The Chief Justice. The one Person everyone pleads to somehow magically appear when there is injustice. The reason we want to talk to Him is more than likely because the injustices perpetrated against us cause us all to have some kind of beef with Him. So there stands the Chief Justice . . . and here come the questions.

"Why does evil prevail?"

"Why can't 'right' get the upper hand in this world?"

"What's the problem? There seems to be so much wrong."

"Who is there to make it better?"

We all know that in the "sweet bye and bye" all things will be made right, but as an old college professor once asked me, "What about in the 'nasty now and now'?"

The world cries out for justice!

The hunger for justice is a well-grounded hunger. No doubt, upholding good and punishing evil keeps a society safe, right? When there is no justice, wrongdoers are released and continue in their ways. When there is no justice, those choosing to do right are not rewarded.

But with all the talk about right and wrong and punishing evil, the elephant in the room that must be addressed is, "Who makes the rules and who defines justice?" One only has to be a parent for a short time to realize this question has to be answered on a scale as small as a family as well as in a global scope, because justice is called for universally.

In an article from Santa Clara University, "Justice and Fairness," it is argued that in an attempt to protect the community as a whole, criminals are punished according to what others find just or right. The article states, "Punishments are held to be just to the extent that they take into account relevant criteria, such as the seriousness of the crime and the intent of the criminal, and discount irrelevant criteria such as race."[14]

Punish evil and reward the righteous. It sounds simple. But the article bears out that justice is not as simple as it sounds. There are relevant criteria to consider, such as the seriousness of the crime and the intent of the accused—each a separate cog pushed into the spokes of the grinding wheels of justice.

This is why I wanted to introduce you to the Chief Justice, the creator of the laws of nature, or what we call natural law. The natural law is a moral theory, which asserts there is a moral code which applies to all humans and which exists within our nature. This moral code is knowable through human reason by reflecting rationally on our nature and purpose as human beings.[15] The Chief Justice wrote that law and left it for His creation in a handbook called the Bible. It is knowable and it is true. In speaking about those who may not believe in it C. S. Lewis writes:

---

14. Manual Valasquez, Claire Andre, Thomas Shanks, S. J., and Michael J. Meyer, "Justice and Fairness," Markkkula Center for Applied Ethics at Santa Clara University, accessed November 15, 2018, https://www.scu.edu/ethics/ethics-resources/ethical-decision-making/justice-and-fairness/.

15. "Natural law," Quizlet, accessed March 4, 2019, https://quizlet.com/78116863/natural-law-flash-cards/.

*Whenever you find a man who says he does not believe in a real Right and Wrong, you will find the same man going back on this a moment later. He may break his promise to you, but if you try breaking one to him he will be complaining 'It's not fair' before you can say Jack Robinson. A nation may say treaties don't matter; but then, next minute, they spoil their case by saying that the particular treaty they want to break was an unfair one. But if treaties do not matter, and if there is no such thing as Right and Wrong—in other words, if there is no Law of Nature—what is the difference between a fair treaty and an unfair one? Have they not let the cat out of the bag and shown that, whatever they say, they really know the Law of Nature just like anyone else?[16]*

When justice doesn't make an appearance right away in a situation we feel calls for it, in our exasperation we tend to call on the works of the flesh. Available in the flesh's kennel are at least two pit bulls known as *Hatred* and *Contentions*. As Proverbs 10:12a confirms, these two will turn on each other to stir up the strife they have already created. Both possess a spirit of rivalry. They are traveling companions riding along together looking for a fight.

The description reminds me of my dad. Before he became a Christian, he and a friend would literally drive around looking for fights. When they saw a couple of guys fighting they would stop and ask, "Is this a personal fight or can anybody join in?" Seriously, they joined a few.

Hatred and contentions do the same. They react quickly to injustice by taking measures into their own hands, believing that will help settle issues faster and more to their satisfaction—because waiting takes too long in their opinion.

> *Hatred and contentions react quickly to injustice by taking measures into their own hands.*

The saccharine continues to be sprinkled on our situations in an attempt to sweeten the harsh but necessary decisions we are about to make. You see, the release of the two pit bulls allows them to show their ugly attitudes by sinking their teeth into our choices. This, in our minds, makes everything right again. In actuality, however, it sustains and intensifies everything that is wrong.

---

16. C. S. Lewis, *Mere Christianity* (New York: Harper Collins, 1952), 6–7.

In the Book of Proverbs, King Solomon juxtaposes the two sides of the justice argument and demonstrates the wide gap between the two: "The righteous care about justice for the poor, but the wicked have no such concern" (Proverbs 29:7 NIV).

There it is.

Staring us in the face is the age-old war between the righteous and the wicked. Wherever this battle started and for whatever reasons it started, the result is that the combat seems to be where our definition of justice emanates.

Set things straight!

Rectify the matter!

An eye for an eye!

Tags back!

## Caught between the Two

Her name is Rita. A prettier girl you may never have met.

She is a charmer.

She is smart.

She is athletic

She is feminine.

She graduated with honors from a private university without the financial help of family. I found myself feeling proud of her, yet for none of the above reasons. I felt proud for her because, on the whole, I noticed that at an early age in her life, she elected to make right choices. You might retort, "That doesn't seem like a reason to be proud. After all, she *should* be making right choices."

But if you knew her background as I do, I believe you would understand. If anyone had a reason not to make right choices, it was Rita. She comes from a broken home. Siblings are now paying for their wrong choices in prison, in relationships gone terribly wrong, and in financial ruin. Her distant, distracted parents seemingly could not have cared less whether she made right or wrong choices.

One day to my dismay, Rita's determination to continue making good choices despite her conditions met a crossroads too great to persevere. I watched her hunger for a rectifying justice grow and become too much to overcome. She believed a lie, and it seemed life had dealt too difficult a hand for her to triumph.

Her countenance changed.

Her attitude began to go south.

I saw her move quickly toward handling reparations on her own. People whom she thought had hurt her needed to pay now, in her opinion. Her justice hunger morphed into voraciousness. The problem was, some of those people had been her greatest supporters, but when a person wants retribution, justice boards no patience in its kennel. Rita gave in to the wrong side of the hunger and sought the works of the flesh to come to her rescue.

And the pit bulls were released.

Those once close to Rita were now distant in her mind and were about to be cut off. A price was about to be extracted from them. She spared no social media vehicle for releasing the dogs of vengeance. And like James 3:16 says, "For where envy and self-seeking exist confusion and every evil thing are there."

*God's idea of justice is a self-cleansing justice.*

The justice hunger Rita began to feed was not the justice hunger placed in us from creation. It was justice with a negative adjective added originating from some dark abyss, not from the fruit of the Spirit.

## FROM THE HEART OF GOD

In an article published in *Relevant Magazine* titled, "What Is Biblical Justice?" pastor and author Tim Keller writes:

*Two words roughly correspond to what some have called "primary" and "rectifying justice." Rectifying justice is mishpat [pronounced mish-pawt]. It means punishing wrongdoers and caring for the victims of unjust treatment. Primary justice, or tzadeqah [pronounced tsed-aw-kaw], is behavior that, if it were prevalent in the world, would render rectifying justice unnecessary, because everyone would be living in right relationship to everyone else.[17]*

A theology of justice flows from the heart of God. However, the justice that flows from His heart is not a slice of the pie known as rectifying justice. Rather, God's idea of justice is a self-cleansing justice. A justice in and of itself that is altogether fair-minded. It is a personal, moral justice that if emulated would

17. Tim Keller, "What Is Biblical Justice?" *Relevant Magazine*, August 23, 2012, https://relevantmagazine.com/god/practical-faith/what-biblical-justice.

righteously influence our individual behavior so much it would permeate our hearts and render a rectifying justice unnecessary.

At creation, God did not create the world so everything would be equal but rather so that everything embraced equity. It is this sort of justice that makes His creation whole: originally perfect! So when trouble comes, God says, "Wait on Me . . . I will repay." Or as He says it in Scripture, "Vengeance is Mine" (Hebrews 10:30).

> At creation, God did not create the world so everything would be equal but rather so that everything embraced equity.

When we submit to waiting on God, we are given the necessary space to deeply search our hearts and get the plank out of our own eye (see Matthew 7:3–5). It's God's way of saying to us, "Count to ten." He is aware of our hunger for justice and desires to help fulfill it. In His command to wait on Him, He offers us the cool head with the assurance He will make things right in us through the fruit of the Spirit.

In Micah 6:8, God's prophet speaks boldly and clearly to all of us: "He has shown you, O man, what is good; and what does the LORD require of you but to do justly, to love mercy, and to walk humbly with your God?"

Although we do not find the English word *justice* in the Micah mandate, we do find the word *justly*, which in the Hebrew is *mishpat*. What Micah is saying here, as we look at the order the words are placed in the sentence, is that before we can "love mercy," we must "do justly." Before we can "walk humbly with our God," we must "do justly." *Justly* . . . meaning we must punish the wrongdoer and care for the victims of unjust treatment. That seems an easier thing to do when it involves finding the culprits and exercising justice toward them. But here when *mishpat* is to be administered to us and by us personally, it becomes a difficult thing to do.

Yes, you read that right. Administered individually. To ourselves. It is a "clean your own house before you try to criticize my messy house" justice. You see, when self-administered, the *mishpat* (punishing the wrongdoer) becomes a *tzadeqah* (living in right relationship to everyone else) kind of justice. Again, when this happens the "rectifying" adjective is not required.

Thus He offers us *longsuffering*.

Longsuffering is what keeps us from committing stupid mistakes, destroying relationships, and making life worse. It is the road less traveled to experience plain old adjective-free justice. The justice of His own heart is what activates God all through the Bible. It guides Him in His judgments on sin and injustice.

At first reading, longsuffering does not seem to fit the fruit of the Spirit. There is love, joy, and peace, which are all extremely desirable. Then comes a word that seems to be the onion in the petunia patch.

*Longsuffering essentially makes space for God's justice to do its reconciliation work through us.*

Longsuffering. *Long . . . suffering!*

Not only does it contain the word *suffering*, but *long* signals an unspecified duration. To the average Joe, the word could actually be a turnoff. It signals the delay of justice more than the service of justice. But nothing could be further from the truth. *Longsuffering* is indeed the enemy of *mishpat*—rectifying justice—but it fits hand in glove with the word *tzadeqah*—living in right relationship to everyone else. Longsuffering essentially makes space for God's justice to do its reconciliation work through us.

## A MUST FOR OUR VOCABULARY

All believers need to ask ourselves three vital questions of faith:

1. Do I truly believe God is in control?
2. Do I truly believe God is good?
3. Am I willing to wait until God can verify to me the answer to the first two questions?

Longsuffering takes on an entirely new meaning with affirmative answers to all three questions. The word even begins to sound comfortable, like a friend and not a competitor to our hunger for justice. Three yesses activate the early stage of our living in a right relationship with our fellow man.

The fact is, none of the justice family named at the beginning of this chapter would ever wait for 1 and 2 to be proven. Joining that family is like mounting a crazy, never-ending hamster wheel. Somewhere, someone or some group will latch hold of one of the adjective children and begin demanding that their brand of justice be administered to all of society whether guilty or not. They believe their hurt is too intolerable to live with or too deep for anyone to ever climb out of. Thus the centrifugal force of the spinning circle tosses us and our longsuffering off the hamster wheel. And those who mount the wheel will tirelessly remain longsuffering-less until some sort of justice is extorted. This is why Jesus' words "vengeance is Mine" must remain in our vocabulary and used as often as our circumstances call for it. Jesus' decree for us to wait on Him leads us to embrace the God-given hunger for justice inside each of us. We then set in motion a mindset to choose the fruit of the Spirit over the works of the flesh every time.

## LABEL THEM WISE

Ken and Becky began on the ground floor of what became an especially successful ministry. They gave their best, even through times where sacrifice was extracted, not volunteered. But that was not a problem to them because they knew where the call of God had placed them. A sacrifice to them was a positive. It actually was a buoyant to their spiritual veracity.

It meant skin in the game.

It meant ownership.

It meant if the ministry became a successful endeavor they would be more than a participant—they would be a partaker in whatever success brought.

Or so they thought.

They had hooked their wagon to someone they believed would do the right thing. One day their belief and their reality collided. The impact was unexpected, unpleasant, and unreal! They discovered that dawning in their hearts was the fact that their world was about to change forever. And indeed it did.

Then came the *whys*.

The *I can't believes*.

The *How did this happens*.

The tears.

The anguish of realizing they had been hoodwinked.

They found the decision to ride it out was not going to succeed. The new leadership had other ideas: a different direction. Their life indeed changed. And . . . I am happy to say, it changed for the better. Having told you their story, let me share with you the interim between "their life changed" and "for the better."

This duo sat in my office not as the "had it made" couple some people thought they were. As their counselor, I heard the hurt flow from their hearts in more than a dozen shades of sorrow. I heard their ideas of reckonings. Some of them were actually very creative. I heard their "we will get them back" scenarios.

I just listened. I knew the quality of this couple, and I knew the chances of their schemes ever coming to completion were at best minimal. Through the sessions I witnessed their hearts move slowly from the shadowy side of the justice hunger to the fruitful side. I must say Ken and Becky were a picture of longsuffering, an example to be followed. I witnessed in their attitudes *mishpat* (a predatory justice) decreasing and *tzadeqah* (a longsuffering justice) increasing.

Today you would never know, unless they told you, that this deep hurt ever occurred. They have been led to an even more globally impacting ministry far beyond the original and far beyond their expectations. They are there, I believe, because they did not make a fatal error in turning the vicious pit bulls loose from the works of the flesh kennel. Trusting in Jesus' promise, "Vengeance is Mine," worked!

Maybe it sounds cheesy or trite, but Becky and Ken found longsuffering does not cost; it pays!

## THE BALL IS IN YOUR COURT

In your quest to fulfill the hunger for justice, where do you turn? What do you think is the right path to take? Which side do you feel will eventually produce the right outcomes for your situation? You have a daily choice. You can be lifted up or you can place yourself in the vortex of a downward spiral. It really is your choice today to descend into the works of the flesh and release the hounds of darkness called Hatred and Contentions. Or you can choose to ascend into the fruit of the Spirit and allow longsuffering to have its way to give space for Jesus' "I will repay" declaration.

HATRED/CONTENTIONS → JUSTICE ← LONGSUFFERING

# CHAPTER 6

# THE HUNGER
# FOR CONTROL

W ho's in charge?
The answer to this question is key to understanding daily
issues of responsibility. The question can formulate itself in
many ways: Who pays the consequences? Who is to blame? To whom are we
answerable? We seek these answers so persistently because responsibility is an
indicator of control, and control is something all of us want.

What many of us don't realize is that our desire to know who's in charge
gnaws at us from a deep inner hunger for control.

Others I have spoken to confirmed with me that control seems to be the
most intense hunger of all. According to them, the instant they sense a loss of
control, an extreme pressure develops.

On the Changing Minds website, D. Siegel wrote about the loss of control
one feels when faced with a serious illness: "One of the most disturbing things
about having a terminal illness, as those who unfortunately suffer from such
afflictions will tell you, is the feeling of powerlessness, of being unable to do
anything about it. Being unable to control the illness and knowing that others
cannot help either can be even more painful than impending death."[18]

Similar to how frustrating it can be when we have lost control of our health, we
can also experience profoundly negative personal and relational consequences

_____

18. D. Siegel, "The Need for a Sense of Control," *Changing Minds* (website), accessed March 4, 2019,
http://changingminds.org/explanations/needs/control.htm.

when we feel we've lost control of our lives—when we no longer feel in charge.

In response to this loss of control, we often desperately scour the landscape for any morsel of information or new technique promising to help us regain it—or at least help us cope without it. Truth is, we all strive to keep from being frighteningly, powerlessly exposed to unworkable crises and unwanted chaos that seem to fill our world.

## A SAGA OF TWO CONTROLS

*Controlling, control issues.* Most everyone today is familiar with these terms. Pop psychology has run amuck, and we all have become diagnosticians, casually affixing these labels to people we observe—even to ourselves.

Most everyone can identify a controlling person by the tight rein they attempt to throw around people and things in every corner of their life. Marriages are threatened when one spouse becomes controlling and seeks to exercise so much control over the union that they smother the other. Parents with control issues stunt the growth of their kids or, as the Bible says, provoke their kids to wrath (Ephesians 6:4) when exercising a stifling control over their surroundings, friends, and choices. And who hasn't felt the tyranny of a boss with control issues, who manipulates subordinates like puppets, or whose idea of delegation is micromanaging every decision?

However, oftentimes the things we feel are critical to control—whether they are spouses, children, employees, or life-threatening illnesses—are the very things we never can control. When we realize we do not have control over these things, this is when the hunger God gave us to feel in control tends to spiral into dangerous territory. There is a simple explanation, however: God never intended us to be in control of these things.

Still, we think if we could just get control of everything or everyone, we could keep the sadness and regrets of life at arm's distance. But when these evils break through despite our best efforts to control our world, we look to another fail safe that promises help in maintaining the order we've worked so hard to establish: God.

After all our attempts to control have failed, we begin searching for who is actually in control, because that is the one we tell ourselves we can blame for our distress.

And since God is sovereign, meaning He is always in control, then He must be the One responsible for all the ugliness crashing onto the shore of our life.

"He could stop it if He is all-powerful as He claims," we reason.

The combustible elements of frustration over our loss of control and indignation over what appears to be God's failure to exercise control begin mingling within us, needing only a trigger to ignite an explosion. So when the unfairness of life or broken promises of people who should have kept their word cascade down on us, sweeping us dangerously downstream like a flood from a broken dam, or when things seem to be falling apart because our expectations are completely unmet, we begin to see the tempting means available to help us restore order.

They are warehoused nearby in the works of the flesh.

Before looking more closely at them, it is important to understand that the scenarios described above reflect an attempt to control people or circumstances. This type of control is a distortion of the hunger God intended us to satisfy; the essential difference between the God-given desire for control and the distorted appetites for control is in the objects we seek to control.

Controlling people and circumstance has never been God's plan for other people. Consequently, that type of order never lasts long nor ends well.

This truth is critical to understand because the object of our control usually determines the means by which we will try to achieve it. Since it's not in God's plan for us to control others, attempting to do so ultimately results in a failure-spiral constantly demanding we intensify efforts so we don't surrender what control we have. Sadly, doing so only deepens our hunger for more and more control. In short, we will never satisfy our hunger for control if we set out to control the people in our life.

*We will never satisfy our hunger for control if we set out to control the people in our life.*

Trying to control our circumstances or the outcomes of every situation we face is equally futile. The end of this futility is predictable, and many have experienced it time and again. When things do not turn out as we had hoped, dreamed, or planned, the frustration within can become overwhelming.

The reason for these lamentable outcomes is because both are trying to control things they never can. They are experiencing a distortion of what the hunger for control was meant to be.

When this happens that warehouse containing the works of the flesh is opened and a couple tools are immediately offered—two handy remedies we've probably noticed seem to work well for others who try to get or maintain control over people and situations. These two are bedfellows; they are light sleepers that wake easily.

Their names are *jealousy* and *anger.*

Jealousy often wakes within us when life seems unfair or others are getting ahead of us or have something or someone we want, providing motivation for us to seize more control so we don't "miss out." Then we discover the only means to capture this control is through anger—keeping people so afraid of our reaction to disappointment or disagreement they will at least appear compliant to our desires.

These negative reactions are usually aimed at family or a relationship. To carry forward the earlier examples, we get angry with our boss, our children, our spouse, or our government for unmet expectations or broken promises, and even when our expectations were unreasonable in the first place.

Many people live believing the emotions of anger and jealousy are a necessity in life. After reading through the beginning of this chapter, perhaps you are asking yourself how the unexpected circumstances and relationships in your life can be controlled or even maintained without anger and jealousy.

Doesn't jealousy in some way keep us striving for more? For better? Without some form of jealousy, what keeps life from being boring? What keeps us chasing the dream?

Likewise, we wonder, isn't the world filled with angry people seeking control? If we shelve our own anger, how can we ever hope to keep from falling under the control of whoever has mastered the use of their own anger?

It is these kinds of questions that employ fear tactics and keep people trapped by blinding them to any alternatives to anger or jealousy. That is why we must look at *jealousy* and *anger* more closely.

## JEALOUSY

Jealousy stems from fear; this fear can be generated either by a situation already occurring or by one that is looming. Another element of jealousy that presents itself is that it isn't a loner, but anger can be.

You can be angry *at yourself,* but have you really ever been jealous *of yourself?* No, because jealousy is typically triangular in shape. To exist and to exercise any control, jealousy requires three entities—your jealousy and two other persons or your jealousy, another person, and a desirable object like a new car, new house, new promotion, an unusual talent or gift, or the latest anything. To complete itself, jealousy is always looking outward at other people or things.

In counseling sessions I have found those talking about their jealousy—whether a victim or offender—tend to frame it directly in terms of control. Jealousy is a useful tool. It helps fabricate strategies of control, like influencing the choices of friends with whom they socialize or controlling where others can and cannot go.

All this smells like some sort of fear of comparison or a worry you might not measure up. So by constantly controlling the situations around you, you squelch any possibility of coming up on the short end of any comparison. Maybe you could look at jealousy as a comely chainmail garment fabricated to cover up and protect your fear of comparisons, and that covering is what makes jealousy so appealing.

> *By constantly controlling the situations around you, you squelch any possibility of coming up on the short end of any comparison.*

If there wasn't a hunger called control, there would likely not be a problem with this part of our depravity. But unfortunately the hunger is long established and timeworn. The death of jealousy and anger, if that indeed is a possibility, will begin only when jealousy and anger have become way too painful or undesirable for one to continue. Or when *a better way* eases, or more hopefully quiets, the gluttonous appetite of your hunger for control.

## ANGER

If all our harmful emotions were ordered on a list, anger would be at or near the top because it is so helpful as a coping mechanism; for this reason alone, it's usually highly valued.

Over the years, anger declares its value in given circumstances by convincing us it will either help us stay in control or gain control of difficult issues; some believe anger is so powerful it can help us overcome the most difficult issues we face.

> *Anger declares its value in given circumstances by convincing us it will either help us stay in control or gain control of difficult issues.*

Anger lulls us into a false belief that it gives us the strength to get through the bad times. It insists it is a source of energy that keeps us from falling apart or into complete despair. Because of its siren songs, anger becomes our constant friend, an anchor, a sort of handyman that fixes anything broken.

Anger has become so prevalent in our culture, an entire industry has sprung up around "managing" it—which usually consists of groups filled with people trying to get a handle on their internal rage and who seek the source of their hostile attitude or why any little incident will trigger their anger. The numbers of people enrolled in this type of therapy have reached levels that make it seem almost fashionable for people to require help taming their rage.

*Can anger really be managed?*

Despite the seriousness of runaway anger, it strikes me as an objective so futile it's nearly amusing: classes to learn how to control what is so powerful it can control us. "Anger management" is a curious term to be sure and raises more questions than answers.

Can anger really be managed? Can the ultimate controller itself be controlled? Perhaps the irony from an actual recent headline can help us answer that: "Man kills man in anger management class."

Managing anger is akin to attempting to keep an inflated beach ball under water. Maybe it could be done for a little while, but eventually it will resurface.

*The works of the flesh are not to be managed. They require forgiveness.*

The word *manage* means to oversee, to hold whatever is to be managed close enough that one may protect and properly appropriate it. In other words, I am to hold my anger close enough so I can control and properly direct it.

It strikes me as strange that socially we are not asked to manage any other of the works of the flesh. Who says, "You need to manage your *fornication*," or, "You should attend classes to manage your *thievery*," or, "You need *revelry* management"? Yet we are intent on managing our anger—keeping it close so we can properly channel it when it inevitably surfaces.

This is the foundational flaw in society's leading solution to the problem of growing rage among its population: The works of the flesh are not to be managed. They require forgiveness.

It makes sense when someone asks our forgiveness for introducing strife into our life; likewise, oftentimes the first thing we seek when we have hated someone or envied them is forgiveness. Why, then, is anger chiefly sought to be managed, not forgiven? Anger is no different from any other work of the flesh, and, as with all the rest, when it is found in our life, we should seek forgiveness for it, not simply attempt to manage it.

## BEYOND FORGIVENESS

"Teresa" sank into the wingback chair in my office. This was the third time she had asked to meet with me this year; each of the first two times had been about the loss of a job.

Because of the note I was handed before this latest appointment, I knew this meeting would be about yet another job loss.

She complained she was mistreated by other staff and was not only passed over for promotions but this time just been let go. The details of her job losses might vary, but we always arrived at the same destination: her anger was raging, and she was having trouble controlling herself.

Teresa found temporary relief in anger management classes before her rage would inevitably come back on her like a Kansas prairie fire. By this point, she had become familiar with the vicious circle but knew no way out.

In the course of our conversations Teresa shared with me that she is an adult child of alcoholic parents. She admitted she had a tendency toward an addictive lifestyle herself but that she stayed away from alcohol because, as she put it, "I do not want to have booze controlling my life the way it did my family."

I explained that alcohol is not the only thing to which people can become addicted. These addictions can range from sleep or food to pornography or shopping.

As I reached for my Bible, I told her the best definition of addiction I've found is in the Apostle Paul's writings to the Roman believers. In regard to his own battles with the flesh, he reveals in the seventh chapter a rare, personal, and yet insightful perspective on addiction: "For I know that in me (that is, in my flesh) nothing good dwells; for to will is present with me, but *how* to perform what is good I do not find. For the good that I will *to do,* I do not do; but the evil I will not *to do,* that I practice. Now if I do what I will not *to do,* it is no longer I who do it, but sin that dwells in me" (v. 18–20).

According to that definition, I suggested Teresa was addicted to her anger.

She agreed; moreover, she admitted not feeling comfortable handling a situation with anything but anger. "When I get angry," she confessed, "I can handle anything!"

Push pause for a second and ponder this. When Teresa began to feel controlled by others (a loss of personal control), she felt her only productive reaction was to get angry. In this, she found an odd comfort in her anger because, without it, she believed others would remain in control of her life, not her.

Teresa's description of how she felt about anger matches others with whom I have counseled. When expressing how anger is generated, people usually describe a negative impetus. There is an action, then a response, which causes another action and another response until the unresolved situation descends to the level where anger is summoned to handle the problem.

I'm not sure Teresa understood what I was trying to say or where I was going with our conversation; the look on her face revealed her confusion. Up to that moment she believed everyone else was responsible for her anger. "If I could just get away from them," she reasoned, "then I wouldn't be so angry."

As I reached to take a sip of coffee, I remembered an illustration.

"Teresa," I said, "If I bumped this cup of coffee that's here on my desk, if I bumped it hard enough, what would spill out?"

With a puzzled look she replied, "Coffee, of course."

"And why would coffee spill? Why wouldn't . . . say . . . orange juice? Or for that matter, why wouldn't Diet Coke spill out of the cup when I bumped it hard?"

"Because coffee is what is in it!"

"Exactly," I said. "So when someone or something bumps your cup hard enough at work, if someone says something, or accuses you, or lets you go, what spills out?"

"Anger," she admitted.

"Well," I continued, "why doesn't goodness or kindness spill out instead of anger?"

She looked down at the Romans 7 passage, placed her finger on it, and replied, "Because anger is what is in me!" The light of truth was rising!

## HE HAS NOTHING IN ME

In John 14, the disciples are sitting with Jesus at the table. He is their King, and, in their minds, He would deliver them from the crushing Roman boot and the suffocating laws of the Pharisees.

In the middle of the evening's conversation, and recorded in the previous chapter of John, Jesus says something that silences them all. He says, "Where I am going you cannot follow Me now" (John 13:36).

Panic ensues.

After He settles them, He says something that could be missed if you are casually reading the story: "I will no longer talk much with you, for the ruler of this world is coming, and *he has nothing in* Me" (John 14:30, emphasis added).

*He has nothing in Me.* This reveals a far more powerful truth than what is understood at first glance.

This tells us in no uncertain terms that nothing was in Jesus except goodness. There was no sin whatsoever within Him that would give Satan an advantage in the visceral events about to unfold.

It also seems to indicate Jesus was confident that neither the circumstance nor the enemy could dictate His response to the ugliness He was about to face because His response was governed by what was "in" Him. And, according to Jesus, nothing was in Him that Satan could use to gain control.

Satan had tried this before during the wilderness temptation, with bread knowing Jesus was hungry and with popularity knowing Jesus had been rejected by His own. These temptations were to satisfy Satan's own twisted desire to exalt himself above God . . . and to be in control.

> *But the enemy had nothing in Jesus. In short, there was nothing evil within Jesus that Satan could bump and spill—no sin whatsoever!*

But the enemy had nothing in Jesus. In short, there was nothing evil within Jesus that Satan could bump and spill—no sin whatsoever!

That got me to thinking: How many times do we allow Satan to place—or how often do we become willing participants ourselves in placing—cups full of the works of the flesh on our emotional tables, only to have them bumped and spilled? Yet there are some who preach that we are responsible for managing those cups, to see to it they aren't bumped. How can we keep a watch on all those cups? Every time we are mistreated, every time we disagree with a circumstance, another cup is filled—another added to the table. Managing them may be possible for a while, but sometime, somewhere, a person or circumstance will sneak up and blindside our table!

> *It's not a matter of managing the contents of the cups; it's a matter of emptying them.*

Anger management is an impossible task. It's not a matter of managing the contents of the cups; it's a matter of emptying them. Jesus

> *If anger is not inside us, then it can't spill no matter how often or how hard we are bumped!*

knew that. If anger is not inside us, then it can't spill no matter how often or how hard we are bumped!

If anger is within you and I do something to trigger your anger, then your anger in turn will create fear in others, as it did for Teresa. Many learn early on they can control people (thereby gaining control of their own life) if they become angry enough to generate fear in others when people don't meet their expectations. Sadly, this usually hurts others badly, both emotionally and sometimes physically.

Anger has many preferred means of satisfying our hunger for control because making others fear our rage seems like a shortcut to the means God has established to meaningfully satisfy this hunger inside each of us.

## THE TWO ARE ONE

Control is a singular hunger of the soul. At first glance, it might seem there is one control for the flesh and one control for the Spirit, but there is only one control; problems begin when this hunger becomes distorted. Trying to control situations and people through jealousy and anger is a distortion of God's intent.

> *God never intended for us to control others or outward circumstances; those are in His purview.*

The works of the flesh promise to satisfy this hunger, but they are only imposters, and a side effect from their use is having control redefined from its original meaning. Once we discover how effortlessly jealousy and anger help us control people and situations, we seek to control them more and more; we become controlling people.

This is the distortion. God never intended for us to control others or outward circumstances; those are in His purview. When we think this way, we are drawn to the expedience anger and jealousy hold out and frequently find ourselves trapped.

Control was never supposed to be so distorted as to need the works of the flesh to solve it. It was never meant to put within us the desire to control somebody else or even to ultimately steal a slice of sovereignty from God to master our own circumstances.

The Scripture exhorts everyone to mastery of self through a vital walk with the Spirit. One of the many such exhortations is found in Galatians 5:16, "I say then: Walk in the Spirit, and you shall not fulfill the lust of the flesh." The proper meaning of control can be clearly discovered in the process of this walk.

The wisdom of the Creator choosing to place within us the hunger for control can be seen in the context of the relationship that walk brings. Controlling our responses to people and situations are the only things that *can* be controlled when it comes to people and situations. Walking in the Spirit is the means we have of securing the fruit of the Spirit. And being in control of ourselves is living proof we know Who is actually in control of all things.

*Controlling our responses to people and situations are the only things that can be controlled when it comes to people and situations.*

Your option is to either choose jealousy and anger or to choose a better way called kindness, to ease your hunger for control of your circumstances. Like choosing what you will wear in the morning, you wake every morning with the option to choose your attitude, what you will think about, and your actions for the rest of the day.

When being in control of others and circumstances or running from being controlled is your highest priority, kindness will always be an afterthought. Our old natures are used to the voices of jealousy and anger, which are always louder than the voice of kindness.

Writing about this in her blog *Inner Bonding*, author Dr. Margaret Paul further explains in her post "Kindness vs. Control":

> *In every interaction with another, we choose our intent, consciously or unconsciously. When our intent is to control and not be controlled, we will create conflict in the relationship. . . . If we do not make a conscious choice to be kind, we may unconsciously choose to control . . . It is certainly easier to remain unconscious of our intent, but this will always keep us stuck and limited in our lives, as well as create our relationship problems. Our challenge is to be awake, aware of what we are choosing.*

> *This will not occur until being a kind and loving human being is*
> *more important than having control over not being rejected or*
> *engulfed.*[19]

In Ephesians 4:31–32 we are given instruction as to what to do and how to choose when that hunger for control makes our empty relational stomach begin to growl and beg to be fed: "Let all bitterness, wrath, anger, clamor, and evil speaking be put away from you, with all malice. And be kind to one another, tenderhearted, forgiving one another, even as God in Christ forgave you."

Nowhere in this or any other Scripture passage will we find that management is the objective for any of these hurtful actions. In fact, we are told the opposite; we are exhorted to put it away from us.

> *Nowhere in any*
> *Scripture passage*
> *will we find that*
> *management is*
> *the objective*
> *for any of these*
> *hurtful actions.*

In the same way that you would certainly throw out a maggot-infested, rotting piece of meat on your kitchen counter, the Scripture says to do the same with anger and jealousy. And what are you instructed to replace them with?

Kindness!

When you finally are convinced that kindness is a better option than either jealousy or anger . . . when you finally get to the point to where you are tired of feeding the control-hunger with them . . . when you finally realize they offer no satisfaction, only more hunger, the Spirit invites you to try a hunger-fulfilling fruit. Similar to the living water that Jesus told the woman at the well about, eating of this fruit promises genuine satisfaction.

Try some kindness.

> *Kindness does not*
> *control; it impacts.*

Kindness does not control; it impacts. Kindness is a fruit produced by the Spirit when we walk with Him and is by definition something given to others. Unlike works of the flesh, however, kindness is beneficial and a blessing to others.

The Spirit offers kindness because it is an inner control. It doesn't seek to control others or circumstances but

---

19. Dr. Margaret Paul, "Kindness vs. Control," *Inner Bonding* (blog), October 31, 2006, http://www .innerbonding.com/show-article/580/kindness-vs-control.html.

rather self. When you try this fruit, you might never hunger for the distorted, redefined control of anger and jealousy again!

Being kind to people in situations where we would rather control people demonstrates we understand the real hunger God has given us and provides an opportunity to acquire everything we seek when attempting to control others and circumstances. Only it does so meaningfully and by means that are anything but controlling.

If the popularity of the terms "anger management" and "rage issues" is any indication, there are many, many people who are choosing to satisfy their hunger for control with jealousy and anger. But these are not the only choices; the Spirit offers kindness.

Exercising kindness demonstrates that not only have we recognized the best way to maintain positive control but we also understand and embrace that control truly rests with God, with whom we can trust our lives, our circumstances, and our souls!

JEALOUSY/ANGER → CONTROL ← KINDNESS

CHAPTER 7

# THE HUNGER
# FOR RESPECT

I f you could turn back the clock to June 3, 1967, and turn on your radio, it is likely you would hear the number-one song of Billboard's Hot 100 singles. Although it was an Otis Redding song, a young African-American girl from Detroit jerked it from his grip and made it her life's signature song. Because of its popularity over decades, even today you will still hear it played. Who wouldn't recognize the strong passionate voice of Aretha Franklin spelling out R-E-S-P-E-C-T.

When one wants to emphasize a point in the course of a conversation, they might spell the word first and pronounce it second. For example, a parent, before doling out a consequence to a kid's defiance, may tell a child, "I am D-O-N-E *DONE* with your attitude!" Spelling it and saying it in the same breath seems to add value to what is being communicated. And so the song struck a chord with millions of people who were living their lives putting one foot in front of the other in the daily routine of getting up, going to work, and coming home week after week, month after month, and year after year. In the repetitiveness of taking care of business, they somehow felt disrespected. Aretha's anthem was like a collective, respect-hungry population saying to whoever needed to hear it, "I want some R-E-S-P-E-C-T *RESPECT!*"

The hunger for respect knows no age, race, or gender barriers. Everyone in the course of developing their God-given talent wants their purpose for living, and they reach toward their dream, accompanied by an admiration rooted in a healthy respect. Even if they temporarily fall short of their goals, it will surely be a foundation of respect that will say to them, "You can begin again."

The hunger for respect at times seems insatiable. It is a comfort food. We need it. We crave it. Perhaps similar to when our physical bodies lack a mineral such as potassium, we find ourselves craving a banana, or fish, or a slice of cantaloupe. When we have been in circumstances where overcoming downheartedness has been challenging, a healthy slice or two of respect may just be what the doctor ordered.

Author Emerson Eggerichs, in his book *Love and Respect*,[20] argues that *respect* is the number-one need of the male species of the human race. Although it does not hold first place in the female, it remains an important component in any relationship. That truth can be seen particularly on occasion in the sports world. Remember the last time you witnessed a quick pregame interview of that basketball player driven by the adrenaline rush that is creating such pregame anxiety he can hardly get the words into a proper sentence? "So, what is your plan as you go out on that court in just a few minutes?" asks the sports reporter while shoving the microphone close to the player's mouth. Does he answer, "We're gonna go out on that court and extract some love from that other team?" Not a chance! "We're gonna go out on that court and extract some RESPECT!" He doesn't use the word "win" or "crush them" or "earn a pay check." He says, "We're gonna get some respect!" Nothing else seems important to him at that critical time except respect. He shows us how this important issue rises to the surface at important moments in our lives.

## CONNECTING ETHICS, ETIQUETTE, AND RESPECT

Ethics, etiquette, and respect. Each of these words rests at the core of our existence. Remove them, and you will remove civility from among the human race. Somewhere in every culture, past or present, each has a concise little motto that, when exercised within the culture, makes living in a community bearable. As believers in Jesus Christ, we are aware of His words in Luke 6:31, "And just as you want men to do to you, you also do to them likewise." Or as quoted in Matthew 7:12, "Therefore, whatever you want men to do to you, do also to them, for this is the Law and the Prophets."

---

20. Emerson Eggerichs, *Love and Respect: The Respect He Desperately Needs* (Nashville: Thomas Nelson, 2004), 18.

Contained inside those two passages lies the critical connection between etiquette, ethics, and respect. Ethics without etiquette become tough, cold creeds that pin your shoulders to the mat mercilessly. Etiquette without ethics becomes a random style of living where one could say anything to another no matter how hurtful as long as it is couched in a soft voice and an accompanying toothy smile. Add respect to ethics without etiquette or respect to etiquette without ethics and respect loses respect. Without both together it becomes self-destructive simply by the individual association. Respect craters because it does not and cannot stand alone. Respect is simply a meaningless word listed among the thousands and thousands in the dictionary if it is not connected to an object. I have a friend who is smart and as ethical as can be, but she has regretful etiquette. Her ethics seem cold and calculatingly cutting without a decorum filter, so the respect she may have gained for her intelligence and ethics dissolves in the wake of her lack.

*Ethics, etiquette, and respect. Remove them, and you will remove civility from among the human race.*

Some say etiquette and ethics have no relationship whatsoever. As Peter Flom puts it, "Ethics is a code for behaving in ways that are ethical, moral, and justifiable. Etiquette is a set of rules for making things go more smoothly. There is no real relationship between them."[21] This rationale is just not good reasoning. Saying there is no relationship between ethics and etiquette is like saying there is no relationship between an automobile and an asphalt road. While it is true they are different in every way, they still need each other for safe course plotting. The paved road makes things much smoother for the vehicle, and without an automobile to navigate on it, there is no need for asphalt roads.

When you have an automobile and a paved road, proper analytics say you have a potential reachable destination. Both ethics and etiquette working together are certain to reach respect. There could be no nobler destination for either. I believe respect toward others when achieved influences our etiquettes, and self-respect when achieved influences our ethics. And without the value of a healthy respect in the mix, one can clearly see the possible damage that could

---

21. Peter Flom, "What is the relationship between ethics and etiquette?" Quora, accessed March 4, 2019, https://www.quora.com/What-is-the-relationship-between-ethics-and-etiquette.

be done to the shape of any relationship. And that truth drives and intensifies our hunger to gain more and more respect.

## MORE THAN A FEELING

Anytime the word *feel* or *feeling* is placed in relationship to other words, it impacts the meaning of the sentence. Such as, "I feel as though I should buy the item I dropped and broke in the local antique shop." The word *feel* provides an adaptable connotation and leaves us with a way out, because tomorrow I may *feel*, for some reason, that it was not my fault. To always just *feel* is to traffic in a fluid emotion. Like a blob of mercury on a table, feelings are slippery and hard to manage.

There are those who would argue that respect, like feelings, is an emotion. That it is made up of a mixture of a few different things. Perhaps someone has a quality you wish to have or once wished to have, but either way, it's a quality in which you happen to be weak. So your respect for that quality in them, since you do not possess it, is identified in you as the emotion of subservience. So instead of respect being an arbiter for goodness, it is relegated as a negative emotion for the sycophantic "have nots!"

*Respect should be a guarded value of a moral society.*

Relegating respect to the low esteem of an emotional feeling is to do it a great injustice. It is much more than a feeling. It is at its core a value, and it should be a guarded value of a moral society. It is a value we as the human race owe our fellow man. And it is a value that individually we all should strive to earn, for to have it in our arsenal of influence results in an immeasurable effectiveness. Is it any wonder then that we possess a ceaseless deep God-given hunger to own it?

Let's not go any further into the profundities of the meanings and results of respect until we identify its two separate but equal attributes. They each are important to the discussion and application of respect into our societal norms. First there is the expression of respect that is an *entitled* feature. Second there is the aspect of respect that is the *earned* feature. Just because we are breathing doesn't necessarily mean we have the right to be respected in all areas of living. In our book *Family Fragrance*, my wife Gail and I differentiate the two so that respect could be more identifiable and relevant in the home. It stands to reason it should be taught and encountered first in the home, since we believe the family unit is the single cell of the body of society. What better place for respect to find its beginning than in the heart of the home? We wrote:

> *Distinguish between the two types of respect and teach both in your home. Entitled respect is when a person is due respect by virtue of position: a parent, employer, teacher, pastor, or peace officer. It has more to do with who you are than what you have done. Scripture gives honor to these positions and parents can model respect for them. Hold those in positions of authority in high regard, although they are not perfect. They may make misjudgments from time to time. By reacting to their misjudgment we can further break down communication and respect toward them—even giving children the idea that all authority is bad or stupid. It is easier to later explain a mistake made by an adult, than to rebuild respect that has been torn down by over-reacting in anger or gossip.*
>
> *Earned respect is when we give respect because of what someone has done or how someone has lived. We gain it through our labor, our service to others, and our performance within the family unit. Earning respect . . . is drawn from the concept of two other words, earnest and yearn. The primary purpose of earned respect then is to strive with earnest effort and yearning to advance or stretch forward as a person.*[22]

Once earned, respect can be the greatest motivator of actions by others around you. It is true people tend to work harder, even work smarter, when they believe in someone they can respect. In order to keep the respect you are either entitled to or have spent precious time earning, you must try your best to help make the people around you successful as human beings. Do what you can to see to it they have the tools they need to optimize any shared goals or objectives. When you give respect, you will receive it in kind. This type of community makes the world go round!

## SATISFYING THE RESPECT HUNGER

Ambition! This is a good stand-alone word. Just verbalizing it has a feel-good ring to it. It brings thoughts of someone with a dream willing to spend whatever energy it takes to see their dreams come true. It is indeed a part of one of the

---

22. J. Otis and Gail Ledbetter, *Family Fragrance: Practical, Intentional Ways to Fill Your Home with the Aroma of Love* (Colorado Springs, CO: Chariot Victor, 2009), 55, 56.

nine positive human hungers to be identified and acknowledged within another chapter later in this book. Although we will see the word again, presently in this chapter it will be accompanied by an adjective, which we will see turns its meaning 180 degrees.

In terms of the word *respect* and how to acquire it, we are going to look at two specific words that will, indeed, bring the one using them perhaps an instant self-gratifying respect. But this type of respect is more like a venomous viper causing any respect gained to turn on us, poisoning our very existence. These words are mentioned in Galatians 5 near the end of verse 20. They are respectively *selfish ambition* and *dissentions*. Ugly words indeed! But what do they mean? Let's bring them out of the dark and strip off each of their masks.

The original Greek word translated "selfish ambition," *eritheia*, is used in the New Testament on many occasions and is interchangeable with several other not-so-good words: self-seeking, rivalry, seeking to win followers, factions, strife, base ambitions, contention, factious. All these notions in some way or another are held in any discussion of the Greek word *eritheia*.

William Vine, in his *Complete Expository Dictionary*, notes that the intent of this word use in Galatians 5 is describing someone seeking to win followers. Their ambition is completely self-centered and their intent seems to be to create factions, thus garnering more followers to increase their tribe.

Looking into the meaning of the Greek word *eritheia*, the word is derived from a day laborer who takes no thought of his employer or coworker's reputations. He works only to gratify his personal self-interests whether they are good or bad. Consequently *eritheia* is the attitude of self-seekers, harlots, con artists, and other people-users. Those who in demeaning themselves and their cause are busy and active in their own interests, seeking their own gain to their own advantage.

Simply stated, *dissention* is the bedfellow of selfish ambitions. Its meaning and intent is to capture and use strategies of divisions, which dishonestly and perhaps even immorally, separate people into pointless and groundless cliques. The essence of the meaning of the word *dichostasia* is "standing apart." If you can be isolated, then the odds are increased that you can be cut from the crowd of believers, to be branded by those with selfish ambitions. It's the old divide-and-conquer tactic.

## RESPECT IS RESPECT

Respect at any cost creates a false sense of admiration. There are those who view any kind of respect as useful to their cause, even if they have to get it by false means. They look at respect the way the old man in the TV commercial looked at motor oil. He looked for any cheap oil brand to put into his clunker car. As he is driving down the road with a stream of black smoke pouring out from the tail pipe leaving those behind him hacking and coughing, he mutters, "Motor oil is motor oil!" For some people, respect is a means to an end and not a life's destination.

The evil one is equally okay with that kind of respect. In fact, it is a glorious weapon to him in his efforts to thwart God's purposes in you. He promotes it because he knows it damages the cause of good on this earth. Truly, he has his Diotrepheses everywhere one looks. (See 3 John 1:9–11.) It is doubtful any local church is without one. Satan has convinced those who envision or crave a respected status that these dissentions and selfish ambitions are golden to that dream.

If you find yourself seeking a respect that has heretofore been dodging you, perhaps you are beginning to realize you have been trafficking in the path of those who believe in a forced respect. I urge you to rethink and reexamine the cause for the pangs of respect hunger you have been experiencing. The works of the flesh will certainly offer you a false solution that at first may feel right but will ultimately bring your world down around you like a house of cards. I have witnessed this in some whom I considered to be my close friends. I watched them come to realize too late that wealth or fame is as much an addiction as any other abused substance that can be named. Respect was found in each of those addictions. Although as fleeting as that kind of respect may have been, they settled for it.

Like Charlie. Charlie came out of a Bible college with a fire in his heart to change the world. Sitting in the classes of passionate teachers lit the fire within him. But there was a problem. During the chapel services, big-time preachers would be invited in to speak. At the time Charlie was fascinated beyond reality. He heard their persuasive messages. He was excited by their ability to reach large audiences. Their tailored suits and their string of admirers waiting in line to shake their hands after chapel enamored him. He talked about it in the dorms often. When he graduated he was going to change the world. The underlying problem nobody saw was that Charlie thought all those *externals* created the respect he thought everybody in chapel had for these speakers. So when he went to a small town and planted a store-front church, he thought the clothes, the vocabulary, and the nice house and cars would bring the respect he would need to succeed—so that one day he would be invited to speak in chapel. Building a church, helping change people's lives, digging deep to challenge the congregation to grow in the Word was important but secondary to building the respect he felt would take him places. Image was forefront. What people think about you, he thought, could be manufactured.

Charlie thus came out of college with a dream to change the world but with a false ideal on how that would be achieved. Today he will tell you that dream faded, and now he is content to just having changed himself. Charlie now has a thriving church. The respect he so desired surrounds him, but he is mostly unaware of it. So how did he come to this conclusion? He will tell you it wasn't those externals with which he was so enamored early on. It is simply by allowing the Holy Spirit to help him focus on the fruit of the Spirit and particularly goodness. Charlie has indeed let goodness permeate his existence.

What selfish-ambitions and dissentions can't do is satisfy the hunger for respect. They can both together and separately lead you as the substitutes to the brink of satisfaction, but they cannot sustain you through the tough times. It is the fruit of goodness that nourishes respect.

What is goodness and what does it look like in real time? Actually, goodness looks a little odd in a dog-eat-dog culture. Kelly Minter, in her book *No Other Gods*, paints a verbal picture of this oddity when she writes, "Peter qualifies his statement about us being peculiar strangers. We'll be strange and alien-like because our good works for Jesus will stand out as so breathtakingly good and different and selfless that those around us can't help but praise God. The extreme goodness of our lives is the peculiar part, setting us apart in distinctive ways." She goes on to explain the effects of the substitutes of goodness. "Fulfilling our sinful desires will snuff out the bright flame of this burning goodness."[23]

The original word for goodness is *agathosune*. The root word *agathos* was used in the Greek culture for goodness at a practical level—practical in the sense of a good result, or a benefit or what we might call a blessing, a moral goodness. I must let you know that the original language does not open up any great insights into this word. It is what it sounds like. It means goodness! We must avoid sowing to the flesh and keep sowing to the Spirit. We do that by allowing God's qualities to be established in us and flow through us to others.

---

23. Kelly Minter, *No Other Gods: The Unrivaled Pursuit of Christ* (Nashville: LifeWay Press, 2017), 44.

God's goodness goes way beyond what may be lawfully right. It goes the next mile to what will benefit and be a blessing to others. In the course of following that trail, a true and genuine respect surrounds one who is mostly unaware it is even there.

## MR. BOWDITCH CARRIES ON

There can be no more consummate illustration than the life of a man who had every reason to fall into a selfish ambitious and dissentious life—but who did not—than Nathaniel Bowditch. In fact, his life is an example of goodness over selfishness.

Nathaniel Bowditch (1773–1838) was the fourth of seven children born in Salem, Massachusetts, to a family with a four-generation history of sea captains. His father became a heavy drinker after his ship was wrecked in a storm off the Atlantic coast, and the family's resulting poverty ended Nathaniel's formal education at age ten—the same year his mother died. At twelve, he was pressured by his father to sign an indenture to a ship warehouse owner who cared for Nathaniel, even though by law Nathaniel would have to ask his permission every time he left the chandlery where he worked. For nine long years, he was provided only room and board with no other compensation.[24]

And yet Nathaniel didn't let his dream of an education die. After a full day's work, in his small attic room—and by candlelight—he taught himself algebra, calculus, and Latin (so he could first *translate* and then *study* Isaac Newton's *Principia*), and then later French using the same method of a grammar, a New Testament, and a dictionary. Scholarly men took a personal interest in him, shared their libraries, and he made his own notebooks copying their books.

Within months of being free from his indenture at age twenty-one, he began the first of five sea voyages. On his maiden voyage, he took on board all his notebooks and books. He was furious when his research found thousands of mathematical navigational errors in Europe's best book of its kind on navigation: British author John Hamilton Moore's *New Practical Navigator*. The book included errors in the tables contributed by the king's royal astronomer as well. Bowditch also found an error in Isaac Newton's *The Principia*. He checked and rechecked thousands of figures and computations. His efforts led him to discover a new and much easier way to work lunars that helped sailors know exactly where their ship was located in the ocean by latitude and longitude.

---

24. If you are interested in learning more about Nathaniel Bowditch, see Jean Lee Latham's, *Carry On, Mr. Bowditch.*

American and British scholars were shocked. He had little education and was not even a college graduate. He continued checking figures on his second and third voyages. By the end of his fourth trip, he had begun to write his own book with accurate information, checked, re-checked . . . and checked again! It was called the *The New American Practical Navigator* and soon outsold any British book on navigation.

Before his fifth and last voyage as captain and co-owner of a ship, he was surprised by being awarded the Masters of Arts degree from Harvard without ever setting foot in a classroom. He would also be invited to join most every scientific and intellectual society in America as well as the Royal Societies of Edinburgh and London and the Royal Irish Academy.

You see, Nathaniel Bowditch was smart, but he was also good. He lived goodness. It was his choice. It was his outlook on life. And his life wasn't easy: early extreme poverty, the Revolutionary War, a hard-drinking father, the death of his mother and closest sister, indentured servitude, the loss of all three brothers at sea, fear of being impressed into service by the British Navy, and most stressful—hearing of the death of his beloved wife while he was at sea. All by the time he was twenty-five. He overcame tragedy by making correct choices. But he also chose to do good to others—even when he didn't have to. You see, beginning with that first voyage, he taught navigation to every sailor on board those ships . . . on his own time. He educated them in mathematics, astronomy, and the use of navigational instruments. He put pride and fire in their bellies. Every sailor on his ship down to the cabin boy could work a lunar with his new method, which usually only captains could do using the old method. Each could be promoted to a first or second mate on their next sail, much to the chagrin of his captain who had to hire a new crew.

At twelve years old when he was indentured, a naysayer predicted the school-master's brightest student would be becalmed—a nautical term describing when the wind is taken out of a ship's sails. But one of his benevolent mentors told him that only a weakling gives up when he's becalmed—a strong man sails by ash breeze. See, when a sailing ship is becalmed and can't make progress, sometimes the sailors break out their oars. They'll row a boat ahead of the ship and tow her. Oars are made of ash, and that's when you sail by ash breeze. In spite of all his trials, Nathaniel Bowditch chose goodness instead of the tempting options of selfish ambition or dissentions. And today his book is still aboard every commissioned ship in the US Navy. The depth of respect toward him one hundred and eighty years later cannot be measured. It came to him through his life choices of goodness.

Nathaniel Bowditch sailed by ash breeze. He was never becalmed.

Bowditch seems to be peculiarly different from most in his trade. He was good. His goodness made his behavior more democratic and not focused on people's "class" or station in life. He taught navigation to all the men on his voyages, not just officers. And he didn't *have* to teach any of them. While he was obviously a genius, I believe it was Bowditch's goodness—not just his intelligence—that set him apart.

If Bowditch's life teaches nothing else, it teaches us that choosing selfish ambitions or dissentions to gain a forced respect is the unreal attempting to become the real. After all, isn't that Satan's game plan? Those two deeds of the flesh are his temporal substitute for the eternal reality of goodness. But today, if you choose it, you can descend into both those works and perhaps even gain some temporary respect. Or you can ascend into the Spirit's fruit of goodness and begin building a great, respected future upon the eternal!

SELFISH AMBITIONS/DESSENTIONS → RESPECT ← GOODNESS

CHAPTER 8

# THE HUNGER
# FOR TRUTH

An unsolvable problem seemed to crop up with the restoration of my 1973 Datsun 240Z sports car. It concerned a certain part that was just no longer available. While speaking to a professional restorer in the city where I attended college, I noticed he began to write down questions. Each would need an answer. It was the answers to those written questions that eventually led him to the solution: a 3-D printer. My problem was solved. The extinct parts the 3-D printer created for my Z-car looked like the original or, better yet, it looked awesome!

The ability to ask a good question brings along with it the skill of learning. The best questions you ask are sometimes more important than the impressive answers you give. Often it is the question that drives you to the solution.

Perhaps the greatest question ever to be recorded in history came from Pontius Pilate. It emerges out of a series of questions recorded in John 18.

"Are you the King of the Jews?" (v. 33).

"Am I a Jew?" (v. 35).

"Are You a king then?" (v. 37).

"*What is truth?*" (v. 38).

While standing before Jesus, when he thought the life of the creator of the universe was in his hands, Pilate asked, "What is truth?" I don't believe this was a rhetorical question. The chaos and confusion rampant in the territories of Rome had whittled away any traditional definition of truth. Everybody had his or her own truth claim. Much like the definitions of what is truth in our culture today, truth had been so diluted it was unrecognizable even to the privileged literati of Pilate's day. So Pilate lets the cat out of the bag by asking what he surely felt was a legitimately difficult question. After all, Jesus had just told him He had come to "bear witness to the truth" (v. 37). My active imagination tells me the look on Pilate's face must have been one of befuddlement. Here Pontius Pilate is a striking illustration of a sentence my mother used to say to people resembling a swift-footed, bobbing, weaving pugilist, truth dodger: "You wouldn't know the truth if it were standing right in front of you."

It is no wonder there is confusion. There are so many definitions of truth no one really knows who to trust when somebody says, "Will the real truth please stand up?" The magazine, *Philosophy Now*, once posited the question, "What is truth?" to its readers and posted several of the responses to their website.[25] Two of those responses stood out to me:

> *Truth is not constant. Some beliefs which were held to be true are now considered false, and some for which truth is now claimed may be deemed false in the future . . . Truth is good for helping us decide how to act, because it serves as a standard for making some sort of sense of a world populated by half-truths and untruths.*
>
> *In the end, even in an entirely materialistic world, truth is just the word we use to describe an observation that we think fits into our narrative.*

What we seem to be hearing today perhaps is what Pilate seemed to be hearing from the culture of his day. What truth is said to be really isn't a universal truth at all. It is more likely an individual belief—whatever one believes. What anyone has personally experienced and deems such to be true, they eventually will bow to it. Those experiences and random beliefs become his or her truth. Now all that needs to be done is to speak it often enough to solidify it as a truth claim. "My truth." So the query "What is truth?" as Pilate puts it, is indeed a justifiably good question.

Perhaps the reason there is so much writing about the meaning of truth is because it is not possible to put the whole of it in a thousand pages much less a single sentence. It is notable that Jesus did not answer Pilate's question in sentence form. In fact, there was an eerie silence punctuated only by the slap of Pilate's sandals on the pavers as he exited the room. But Jesus had given the

---

25. "What Is Truth?" Question of the Month, *Philosophy Now*, accessed November 20, 2018, https://philosophynow.org/issues/86/What_Is_Truth.

answer to His disciples in a succinct sentence when the chips were down in the upper room. Jesus told the twelve He was leaving them and where He was going they could not immediately follow. When Thomas blurted out that the group did not know the path to get to where Jesus was going, Jesus laid it all out in a sentence. "I am the way, the truth, and the life" (John 14:16). Simply said, truth resides not in an axiom about truth, but in the person of Jesus Christ.

*Truth resides not in an axiom about truth, but in the person of Jesus Christ.*

The hunger for truth resides deeply within us. I am sure that rings true to you. Perhaps there is something deep within you even as your eyes pass over this sentence for which you crave the truth. Maybe it's a problem that has dogged you for months. Maybe it's a Scripture passage that haunts you so much because you can't grasp its depth. Perhaps you sense a close friend is caught in some sort of deception, and the truth hunger is profoundly noticeable inside him. You want him to taste the truth: to take a bite out of the faithfulness fruit that leads to the satisfaction of that deep hunger. You see, the greater the deception is in our world, the greater the craving is for truth. With the rampant deception in the public arena of the world, no wonder we are so hungry. God put that truth hunger inside us.

In 2015 my wife and I traveled to Russia. We were invited to take part in a cultural exchange concerning the role of and condition of the family in our world today. We were given the green light to share our family ministry resources with some pastors and laypeople who had been invited. We gathered in a meeting room in a cultural center that sat about three hundred people. The meeting started on Friday evening and lasted all day Saturday. So on Thursday evening before the conference began, I asked to meet with the pastors of the churches in that area. After I had shared what family ministry might

*The greater the deception is in our world, the greater the craving is for truth.*

look like in their churches, I made a statement concerning some newfound religious freedoms in their country. I asked how those might affect their ministry to families. In the course of the conversation, the dialogue drifted toward the apparent deception of folks within the Christian community. The pastors were heartsick about the apathy leeching into the hearts of their people. After a few intense minutes, one pastor laid his heart right out on the table around which we were conferencing. He said, "I prefer the church under persecution rather than the church under freedom."

There was immediate agreement around the table: total unity in that statement.

"*Huh?*" was the only word that came out of my mouth.

I was shocked! I'm sure the astonishment was smeared all over my face.

He continued, "Under freedom, we *do* church . . . but under persecution we *are* the church."

A long silence followed.

The hunger for truth was demonstrable in the room. By abandoning what they perceived as fabricated methods to do church, they now choose rather to live and become truth. Whatever it costs.

I will never forget it!

The Word, like a 3-D printer, had faithfully mapped out and formed foundational truth in the hearts of those Russian pastors, and they were voicing it. They had to follow its leading.

## THE TRANSIENT WORK OF HERESIES

*Heresy.* It's an ugly word isn't it? It also has an ugly meaning. It embodies a defective, chosen course of thought and action. Six times it is used in the Book of Acts. Five of those times it is used to connote a sect, a certain group of people (5:17; 15:5; 26:5; 24:5; and 24:14), while one time it is used as a fundamental error in doctrine (24:14). In 1 Corinthians 11:19; Galatians 5:20; and 2 Peter 2:1, it is used in the context of the fundamental error, deceptively and dangerously infiltrating the gathered believers.

> *But there were also false prophets among the people, even as there will be false teachers among you, who will secretly bring in destructive heresies.*
> *—2 Peter 2:1*

That is how the work of the flesh functions. Heresy is the enemy of truth. And it knows it is not as powerful or enduring as truth, so it has to find a way to survive. It has to discover a different way of attacking. Like a cancer cell roaming the body, when it comes in contact with the immune system, it sends out a signal to the healthy system designed to destroy it that says, "Don't hurt me. I'm not harmful. I'm one of you." And the immune system believes it. Fooled, the good soldiers of the body back off the deadly cell, leaving it be. That scenario is what is baffling to researchers. They find themselves helpless to fix it. And left to itself, the cancer eventually destroys the entire body.

Oddly enough there is always a portion of truth in every heresy. That is what makes it attractive. "Don't hurt me. I'm not harmful. I'm one of you" is what makes it treacherous. If it looked like a total falsehood, it would, of course, be rejected out of hand. But the amount of truth it carries within it makes it look friendly. It hopes the truth will recognize and relate to the little amount of common-ground truth inside it and possibly back off, allowing it to destroy the entire body of truth.

*There is always a portion of truth in every heresy. That is what makes it attractive.*

Second Peter 2:1 bears out the veracity of the reported dangers of heresies. It is brought in among people of growing faith who have matured in their faith to be as strong as the faith of the apostles. These people are gathering to continue to strengthen their faith. However, Peter warns of wickedly damaging heresies, half-truths that bring about swift destruction. So be careful! Many will follow their ways, but it's a trap. Guard your heart. Allowed into the life of a person, heresies will dismantle the truth they have built up. The works of the flesh introduce tempting alternatives to the fruit of the Spirit. But those who listen to and heed its claims of "I'm one of you," ultimately end up as confused as Pilate. Perhaps they will find themselves asking similar mocking questions like, "Are you a king?" and "What is truth?"

*Allowed into the life of a person, heresies will dismantle the truth they have built up.*

In his book series A Song of Ice and Fire, author George R. R. Martin writes, "People often claim to hunger for truth, but seldom like the taste when it's served up." Maybe we could even say they seldom like the taste and find it hard to swallow. They may put it in their mouths—even chew on it a little. But like my daughter Becky in her preschool years, after a couple spoonfuls of vegetables, she would suddenly need a bathroom break to secret away the unswallowed veggies. And at the time, I couldn't really blame her. I had trouble swallowing brussels sprouts and asparagus too, but I couldn't employ the same tactic as Becky. A grown man taking that many trips to the loo would be puzzling.

The truth is indeed often bitter to the taste when served with spoonfuls of doubt or disbelief. The point is, truth should not be mixed and served like a cold smoothie with anything on the cultural kitchen counter mixed in. Like a sweet pineapple from Oahu or Maui, truth ought to be tasted unaccompanied, bite after bite. Although at times, a mouthful of truth can be cold enough to give us a paralyzing brain freeze if we swallow it too quickly. Eventually we learn how to take it all in and satisfy our truth hunger relatively pain free.

Pain free? How does that happen?

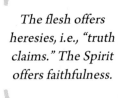

*The flesh offers heresies, i.e., "truth claims." The Spirit offers faithfulness.*

It may at first sound Pollyanna-ish, but it really isn't. God has provided the perfect antidote for the possible pain of truth. It is a Spirit fruit called *faithfulness*. The flesh offers heresies, i.e., "truth claims." The Spirit offers faithfulness. Heresies are an anesthetic. An anesthetic numbs the pain. Anyone who has had an encounter with a venomous spider or snake does not automatically or hysterically look for an anesthetic. At a critical moment like that, numbing the pain could be a fatal mistake. The search instead would be a straightforward quest for an antidote. And not just any antidote. The search would be for a remedy designed for a specific venom. A rattlesnake antidote wouldn't work for a venomous brown recluse spider bite.

Faithfulness is not an anesthetic. It is an antidote. An antidote counteracts or cancels the poison causing the pain. The problem with anesthetic heresies is that they have to be applied again and again . . . over and over until the cause of the pain is hopefully masked.

## A FLAWED CURE VERSUS THE ENDURING FRUIT OF FAITHFULNESS

I want to introduce you to Georgiana and James. They are not a couple. They live in the same city, but chances are they do not even know the other exists. They come from different cultural, gender, and generational backgrounds. But they are so much alike when it comes to the hunger for truth. And certainly, both are hungry for the truth. Perhaps their problem is that Georgiana and

James both have a lot of friends. Having a lot of friends shouldn't seem like a problem. But their friends are aware of the myriad difficulties each has because both Georgiana and James are serial talkers. Neither owns a pause button or a "what's-appropriate-to-share" filter. Each also has a bag packed full of excuses as to why their lives don't work and reasons why everyone else's does. So because they think everyone else's lives work, their bag is also stuffed with everyone else's truths. What they have been asked to believe to be truth by leisure-time "friend counselors" pegs the heresy indicator needle to the limit.

I have separately shared with each the antidote to poisonous heresies like abortion, same sex marriage, the hook-up culture, divorce, human suffering, and biblical veracity issues. We have sat together through discussions of biblical principles, scriptural truths, historical evidences, and illustrations as to where solutions lie. While sitting in the office it makes sense to them. I see their eyes saying, "This will work. Think I'll try it." But when they walk out the door and mix again with their many difficulties and friendships, they inevitably choose the flawed cure. Each would happily apply anesthetic to numb their pain until the next poisonous hurt. But no worries! They have more anesthetic; but as of yet, neither has tried the antidote. It is indeed a frustration.

*Faithfulness is the fruit that will most preserve truth.*

Sadly a person can decide to wait out the pain until he or she becomes comfortable living with the pain. Many do! It is not impossible that they could even decide to let the cause of the pain regrettably take their life. I have experienced that ugliness too.

This component of Spirit fruit, in contrast, is a large one. Like a watermelon beside a kiwi, faithfulness towers over most of the other fruits. It towers not in its importance but girth. Faithfulness, like love, should sweepingly permeate every human activity to its core. Then faith with love can cut a wide swath within every individual's purpose where hope can break through and blossom. Faithfulness is the fruit that will most preserve truth. Faithfulness is God's version of a 3-D printer shaping and molding His truth generation after generation.

Before the foundations of the earth, God loaded His software into the fruit of faithfulness to carry out His plan. Truth leaps out of the faithfulness of the ancient scribes who took pains to copy every jot and tittle by hand to deliver an uncorrupted manuscript of God's Word. It resided in the faithfulness of the ancient prophets who declared His Word to their generation and faithfully prophesied truth even on threat of death. The Spirit escorted it through faithful apostles who sacrificed everything to get redemption's plan truthfully articulated for future generations. Because of their faithfulness, generations after them could benefit from their Holy Spirit-moved knowledge and then faithfully declare to their children the wonders of His love!

Conceivably you are wondering why I'm comparing great faithfulness to the likes of a mechanical, modern 3-D printer. What could one possibly have to do with the other? Their similarities rest in their functions on the operational level.

> *Faithfulness isn't an event. It is a lifelong process.*

A 3-D printer creates thousands of tiny little slices and builds them to create a complex, solid object just like the original it is patterned after. By building from the bottom up, slice-by-slice, 3-D printers can even create functional moving parts like chains and hinges. But primary to the building up, the operator must take watchful precautions to create a proper foundation: a build plate on which the object to be shaped sits. Without proper care of the plate, the object will warp and become malformed.

Faithfulness has a corresponding function. It takes slice after slice of truth over time and begins to work from the bottom up, building us up in our most holy faith. (See Jude 1:20.) Each layer is a complexity of moving parts that finds its function as members of one body. Faithfulness isn't an event. It is a lifelong process. He who has begun the good work will faithfully preform it. Slice by slice He melds us together! "For precept must be upon precept, precept upon precept, line upon line, line upon line, here a little, there a little" (Isaiah 28:10). We are being built up into a spiritual house so we may faithfully proclaim Him who called us out of darkness to light, out of heresies into faithfulness to satisfy our hunger for truth!

## WARNING: REVERSING POLARITY

The truths we learned as a child of faith won't crumble all at once. But when in the search for truth we encounter someone—a professor, a mentor, a skeptical or agnostic friend—who traffics in heresies, we risk reversing the polarity of the truth printer. What once was being built up now begins to be stripped away slice by slice, line by line, and precept after precept. Such is the story of Jodi. Having been treated like a queen (her words) by her wealthy husband, she walked away from their life of faithfulness. Somehow the polarity was reversed. She crossed the verity line into a different truth . . . her truth. And her truth was all that mattered. Slowly biblical truth was stripped from her foundational beliefs. Little by little, almost unnoticeably stripped away at first. Then like a driverless car coasting downhill gaining a faster pace, she began to experience the need to numb the pain. Unfortunately, her new truth path led her to the bank where she emptied out family accounts and went straight into the arms of a long-distance trucker. Her polarity reversal was stark. The truth is, the road ended with Jodi being fatally shot while lying face down on asphalt, under a car, hiding for her life because of a drug deal gone wrong.

## STEPPING INTO THE GAP

Because of the subject matter of this chapter I am compelled to add this entreaty. Perhaps you have sensed a reversal of the truth polarity in your life. Once there was a faithfully solid foundation upon which precept upon precept, line-by-line, truth was being built up in you. But now there is a feeling of anxiety inside you from some hunger search that could be taking you in a downward trajectory close to crossing the verity line like Jodi.

A different truth claim is badgering you, trying to elbow its way into your life. So maybe it's time to stop and enter into a time with God. A moment of reflection and renewal, just between you and Him.

If that is so, take a few minutes to define your hunger for truth in a prayer journal, identifying how the work of the flesh is acting against the truth inside you. As you spell out the issues, check the appendix for this chapter for Scripture passages that can help you define how faithfulness can better satisfy your hunger for the truth.

You may find that focusing on Scripture and your relationship with God can lead you to the very truth you crave.

HERESIES → TRUTH ← FAITHFULNESS

# CHAPTER 9

# THE HUNGER
# FOR ACHIEVEMENT

W ithin you this very moment is something you've never heard of but is relentlessly driving you through each day. I'd wager you've never been tested for this, but it can be observed, measured, and studied; its effects in our lives are universal and undeniable.

It even has a technical designation: N-Ach.

It looks like a chemical compound, but N-Ach is actually part of something called the Three Needs Theory, articulated by American psychologist David McClelland in the 1960s. McClelland's Need Theory addresses how people are motivated and its implications in the workplace; he proposed that everyone is driven by three needs, and while an individual may be primarily driven by only one, each need is present in every person.

The three needs in his theory are: power (N-Pow), affiliation (N-Affil), and achievement (N-Ach). McClelland, however, wasn't the first person to observe this need for achievement in people. His theory was an expansion of foundational work completed thirty years earlier by noted Harvard psychologist, Henry Murray.

Murray's accomplishments and accolades are difficult to condense. At Harvard, he introduced psychoanalysis to the curriculum and became director of the Harvard Psychological Clinic where he pioneered numerous theories of personality, including personology, which aims to explain present behavior by reconstructing an individual's past life experiences.

His time at Harvard was interrupted by World War II when he served in the Office of Strategic Services (OSS), the predecessor of the current CIA. During this time, his theories on personality were used to help select US and British secret agents, and perhaps of even more significance, he also collaborated on the OSS's personality profile of Adolf Hitler. Among other things, this study accurately predicted Hitler would choose suicide over capture should Germany face defeat and represented the fundamental work in what we know today as criminal profiling.

Dr. Murray returned to Harvard after the war, continuing to research and conduct experiments. Upon retirement, he was named professor emeritus, earning both the Distinguished Scientific Contribution Award from the American Psychological Association and the Gold Medal Award for lifetime achievement from the American Psychological Foundation.

Standing at the front of this man's seemingly inexhaustible works and accolades is his observation of N-Ach—our need for achievement. However, just like Murray observed this need thirty years before McClelland elaborated on it, our need for achievement was alluded to by the Apostle Paul nearly two thousand years before Henry Murray.

The central idea of this book is that the hungers implied by the contrasting lists in the fifth chapter of Galatians are hardwired into our natures by God. We shouldn't be surprised then, to find here allusions to a hunger for achievement that even noted psychologists have concluded is universal within each of us.

To understand this hunger for achievement, we must first differentiate between it and ambition. Essentially, achievement is the fruit of ambition. Writing in *Christianity Today*, Richard Exley conceded, "Without ambition nothing of significance is ever achieved."[26]

Ambition, however, has frequently been considered corrosive. As far back as Aristotle, it has been corralled into categories, marking off healthy ambition from destructive ambition. The philosopher himself labeled virtuous ambition as "proper ambition" and the destructive kind as simply, "ambition";[27] this pure type is where we get terms like *naked ambition* or even *blind ambition*.

Those labels recognize the dark side of ambition, which is untempered by empathy and unconcerned about anything that doesn't serve its purpose; indeed, those terms always reference ambition that has steamrolled people in careers or created suffering within a family.

Christianity has observed this characteristic and historically broad-brushed ambition as inconsistent with God's will. Author Dave Harvey, in his book,

---

26. Richard Exley, "Taming Ambition," *Christianity Today*, May 19, 2004, https://www.christianitytoday.com/pastors/leadership-books/dangerstoils/mmpp05-3.html.

27. Neel Burton, MD, "Is Ambition Good or Bad?" *Psychology Today*, November 16, 2004, https://www.psychologytoday.com/us/blog/hide-and-seek/201411/is-ambition-good-or-bad.

*Rescuing Ambition*, notes that church leaders stretching all the way back to Augustine considered ambition inextricably linked to earthly glory and fame; they considered ambition, he says, in the company of "pretty slimy stuff."[28]

However, while true, this perception of ambition tells only half the story. The other half concerns countless good things and breathtaking achievements that have enabled cultures to prosper, lifespans to increase, and broadened knowledge that trickled down to advancement after advancement benefiting humanity. Psychologist Neel Burton went so far as to suggest, "Many of man's greatest achievements are the products, or accidents, of their ambition."

Ambition is nothing less than that which makes us all strive for any kind of achievement. Again, Harvey defines ambition as "the instinctual motivation to aspire to things, to make something happen, to have an impact, to count for something in life."[29]

This is the love/hate relationship we have with ambition. Without it, achievement is impossible, and achievement is a hunger we all have; yet ambition often runs amuck in the pursuit of achievement, leaving a rabble of victims in its wake.

So is ambition something that must be quashed whenever its influence is felt, or can it be harnessed to serve nobler purposes? These are the questions answered in the lists we're considering. The fruit of the Spirit shows us how to meaningfully and completely satisfy the hungers within, and the deeds of the flesh are held out as counterfeit shortcuts that will never satisfy.

Within the roll call of fleshly counterfeits in Galatians 5 is both envy and murder. These are two powerfully emotive words and are frequently linked together in dark ways; let's look at how they relate to this hunger for achievement, beginning with envy.

## MOTIVE

Motives move us; think of envy as a motive. Motives are the driving forces behind any course of action and can be both good and evil; among the evil ones people are frequently driven by is envy, which is irredeemable.

In its basest form, envy has been defined as, "a feeling of discontent and ill will because of another's advantages, possessions, etc.; resentful dislike of another who has something that one desires."[30]

---

28. Dave Harvey, *Rescuing Ambition* (Wheaton, IL: Crossway, 2010), 14.

29. Harvey, *Rescuing Ambition*, 12

30. Merrill Perlman, "Covetous: The Difference Between 'Jealousy' and 'Envy,'" Visual Thesaurus, March 21, 2013, https://www.visualthesaurus.com/cm/wc/covetous-the-difference-between-jealousy-and-envy/.

Don't confuse envy with jealousy. Among their differences, jealousy is always about what we believe is rightfully ours while envy is centered on a desire for something we don't have or can't acquire. In fact, this definition reveals envy is personal in that it not only desires what we don't have but dislikes those who do have what we desire, believing them to be unjustly advantaged over us.

While envy and jealousy are different motives, envy and covetousness are practically synonymous. As motivations, envy and covetousness are so destructive that warnings and prohibitions regarding them go all the way back to the Ten Commandments in the Book of Exodus because they not only desire things but they also create a warped, negative impression of people in the process. Is it any wonder Solomon called envy, "rottenness of the bones" (Proverbs 14:30 KJV)?

## ENVIOUS AMBITION

Most of us learn early on certain household products must never be mixed. Some of the most dangerous compounds are produced from combining ordinary and even useful items. World War I doesn't seem to have much to do with household safety, but the festering trench warfare in France helps us understand why the warning is passed from generation to generation.

WWI has stood in history as the most prolific example of chemical warfare. In its first use of large-scale chemical weaponry, Germany launched 160 metric tons of chlorine gas in 1915. These menacing, yellow clouds affected the eyes, ears, nose, and throat of entrenched troops and at high doses caused death by asphyxiation; the effects were so cruel, even German officers described chlorine gas as a horrible weapon.

So horrible were they that after the war, the Geneva Protocol was adopted to ban the weaponized use of all lethal gasses. Having witnessed their terrifying savagery firsthand, nearly every country involved in the Great War signed the protocol.

And yet, one of the most gruesome chemical weapons ever deployed in combat and banned by world conventions can be easily created from rummaging through the cupboards of practically any house in America. All it takes is some vinegar and bleach.

Separately, vinegar and bleach are useful for everything from laundry to dissolving hard water deposits on plumbing to even dying Easter eggs. However, when combined, they are extremely volatile and produce the same toxic gas used in the trenches of WWI. Sometimes, incredibly poisonous toxins are created from otherwise benign items.

Think of envy and ambition as being as volatile as bleach and vinegar. By itself, ambition requires great diligence to keep from becoming destructive, but when rooted in envy, something diabolical is birthed that stops at nothing to get ahead or lay hold on what it desires. This fleshly counterfeit motivation cuts ambition loose on everyone around us; often, the people we care about most are the first in a long line of victims churned in its wake.

## MEANS

When the leaders of Israel dumped Jesus on Pilate's doorstep for judgment, Matthew 27:18 tells us, "[Pilate] knew that [the leaders] had handed Him over because of envy." Pilate recognized the sinister presence of envy-fueled ambition in the leaders' supposed indignation. Going back even to Genesis, we find envy present at the first murder. Cain envied God's approval of his brother Abel so much his envy quickly turned to anger and ultimately resulted in bloodshed.

Perhaps Cain felt that by killing his brother he would have no competition for the approval he envied so much, and it would become his by default. Cain's ambition for God's approval didn't lead him to listen more carefully or obey more completely; it seized the shortcut of envy, which concluded the most efficient means to achieve God's approval was to eliminate the competition for it.

Centuries later, the leaders so envied Jesus' popularity they came to believe the devotion of the people would be theirs once more only if Jesus was condemned. Instead of considering their ways or the message He preached that generated such grassroots fervor, envy of Jesus' place in people's hearts mixed with their pure ambition to rule, and a murderous plot was hatched that ended with Jesus nailed to a Cross.

In both cases, envy drove people to conclude that the best means available to finally achieve their desires was murder. In our lists, murder follows envy because means always flow from motives. If it were written as a mathematical equation, it might look like this: Ambition + Envy = Murder.

This evil equation comes to life when we remember, biblically speaking, murder is not confined to actually killing a person. Jesus expanded the definition in the Gospels and warned that murder's precursor emotions, like unjustified anger, are deserving of the same penalties normally reserved for those who are convicted of the actual crime:

> But I say to you that whoever is angry with his brother without a cause shall be in danger of the judgment. And whoever says to his brother, "Raca!" shall be in danger of the council. But whoever says, "You fool!" shall be in danger of hell fire.
>
> —Matthew 5:22

In his biblical commentary, Matthew Henry characterized this expansion of the definition of murder as "heart-murder." He understood Jesus' teaching to indicate that a person experiencing such anger "would kill if he could . . . he has taken the first step towards it."[31]

Commentator Albert Barnes agreed: "The Jews considered but one crime a violation of the sixth commandment, namely, actual murder, or willful, unlawful taking life. Jesus says that the commandment is much broader. It relates not only to the external act, but to the feelings and words."[32]

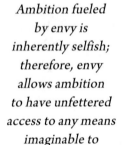

*Ambition fueled by envy is inherently selfish; therefore, envy allows ambition to have unfettered access to any means imaginable to achieve one's goals.*

The Apostle John put it much more bluntly in 1 John 3:15 when he said, "Whoever hates his brother is a murderer."

Whether in the commentators' thoughts or the clear words of Scripture, *murder* as used in the Bible goes beyond taking human life and includes the dehumanizing emotions associated with it. Unjust anger seething against another is not just incompatible with a faith founded on forgiveness, it also foments the attitude necessary to justify treating people with grave indifference and callousness in the pursuit of our achievements.

Ambition fueled by envy is inherently selfish; therefore, envy allows ambition to have unfettered access to any means imaginable to achieve one's goals. The apostle's words in James 3:16 (NIV) corroborate this concept, "For where you have envy and selfish ambition, there you find disorder and every evil practice." This is because envy and murder always come as a package of motive and means. Whether it is things, reputation, or love and acceptance, if envy is the motivation fueling our

---

31. Matthew Henry, Zondervan NIV Matthew Henry Commentary, ed. Rev. Dr. Leslie F. Church (Nashville: HarperCollins, 1992). Accessed November 28, 2018 via Google Books.

32. Albert Barnes, *Notes on the Bible*. Accessed November 28, 2018, http://www.sacred-texts.com/bib /cmt/barnes/mat005.htm.

ambition to acquire them, we will eventually turn to "murder" as a means to achieve the goal of securing it. This combination always results in the destructive ambition so many people have experienced.

Remember Henry Murray, the man who observed our universal hunger for achievement? There's no doubt the brilliant psychologist's achievements have benefited countless people; from his pioneering work in studying personalities to his service in WWII, all of us have probably felt the impact of this man's ambitions to advance in his field.

Unfortunately, Dr. Murray is also notable for a number of more regrettable studies.

Project MKUltra was a secret CIA program that explored methods of mind control by a variety of means, including torture and administration of illicit drugs, and became nearly synonymous with the illegal use of LSD, often given to subjects unwittingly.

This clandestine program is blamed by at least one family for the death of their father when he jumped out a window nine days after CIA agents spiked his drink with LSD without his knowledge. Its methods of research were so far outside the bounds of ethics and civil rights that all documents related to MKUltra were ordered destroyed by CIA director Richard Helms in 1973.

Among the worst of these unethical elements of MKUltra was that its experiments were conducted not in government facilities but rather in hospitals, prisons, and college campuses. Harvard University was one of these campuses, and many suspect Dr. Murray was on the CIA's payroll conducting MKUltra experiments on students without their full knowledge.

While this is difficult to prove conclusively because of the destroyed documents, one person convinced of its truth is David Kaczynski, the brother of Ted Kaczynski. You may recognize Ted Kaczynski by his notorious nickname, the Unabomber.

Ted Kaczynski was enrolled at Harvard as a math prodigy when he participated in a study carried out by Dr. Murray. During the study, participants were traumatized in a variety of cruel ways in order for their reactions to be observed. Among other things, this involved assaulting the most deeply cherished beliefs of the individual; Dr. Murray himself characterized these experiments as, "vehement, sweeping, and personally abusive."

Only age seventeen when the experiments began, Kaczynski became increasingly withdrawn and eventually retreated to a cabin in Montana, dropping out of society altogether. Altogether, that is, except for the sixteen bombs he mailed or hand-delivered that injured twenty-three people and killed three.

How did a teenage, Ivy League math genius become what one person called, "the most intellectual serial killer the nation has ever produced"?[33] Some point to the sadistic CIA experiments young Ted Kaczynski participated in as the genesis of the Unabomber he would become.

MKUltra was initiated less than ten years after Germany's defeat in WWII. Yet, its experiments were conducted in what David Kaczynski himself described as "a scientific culture that failed to learn and recoil from the grotesquely unethical conduct of Nazi scientists who treated human subjects with no more empathy than they would have treated an inanimate object."[34]

At the helm of those "grotesquely unethical" experiments at Harvard is the man who first observed N-Ach, Dr. Henry Murray. Dr. Murray's need to achieve greater understanding about human beings was at times sadly driven by a destructive, selfish ambition that justified "murdering" the very humanity of the humans he had dedicated his life to help.

James's warning about the flesh's shortcuts to achievement are often sadly demonstrated in our society. Indeed, where selfish ambition is found, every evil work lurks nearby.

## COUNTERINTUITIVE

*Jesus came to set us free from such norms; His way is counter-everything.*

Envy-fueled ambition screams at us to get ahead and achieve no matter the cost involved. Looking at our society, it's easy to conclude that is indeed the law of our particular jungle.

However, Jesus came to set us free from such norms; His way is counter-everything, especially counterintuitive. For example, when Jesus told His disciples, "The first will be last" (Matthew 20:16 NIV), and that the greatest among His disciples would be servant of all (Matthew 23:11), He advocated a unique, yet effective, path to greatness.

In opposition to envy and murder, the flesh's avenues of achievement, the Spirit offers the fruit of gentleness. You'll search long and fruitlessly for a book on achievement through gentleness. And it certainly won't be written by decorated generals or

---

33. Alston Chase, "Harvard and the Making of the Unabomber," *The Atlantic* (June 2000), https://www .theatlantic.com/magazine/archive/2000/06/harvard-and-the-making-of-the-unabomber/378239/.

34. David Kaczynski, "Ted and the CIA, Part 2," *Times Union*, December 29, 2010, https://blog.timesunion .com/kaczynski/ted-and-the-cia-part-2/285/.

captains of industry. Gentleness as a means to achievement is as deeply counterintuitive as greatness being achieved by servanthood.

The primary ideas behind the word *gentleness* is submission to authority and consideration of others. These are not the character traits we typically expect to find in high achievers. Submission and consideration seem more like the character traits of doormats.

Gentleness in the Bible, however, is never associated with weakness; rather, it's often described as an irresistible force. Scripture says a gentle answer is strong enough to turn away anger (Proverbs 15:1) and powerful enough to overcome stubbornness and break bone (Proverbs 25:15).

*Gentleness is not an imperative for Christians to underachieve; rather, it's a counterintuitive means to achievement that is richly satisfying.*

Gentleness is not an imperative for Christians to underachieve; rather, it's a counterintuitive means to achievement that is richly satisfying.

Our hunger to achieve is given to all of us by our Creator; therefore, we know achievement is neither evil nor is it limited in scope to so-called "Christian" goals. Our hunger is not to achieve particular things; we hunger to achieve meaningful things.

Scripture does, however, exhort us to be wise in choosing the achievements we pursue and sensitive to how we pursue them. These are two indispensable considerations gentleness helps us navigate.

## DISCERNING THE VALUE

We must always discern the actual value of any achievement we pursue. How is that done? First, we must understand that anything we achieve in our life that is not of direct, unquestioned eternal value (such as a promotion or even fame) is an earthly achievement and will ultimately fade.

After chronicling the sweeping saga of American General George Patton's exploits in WWII, the movie *Patton* draws to a close with the general walking into the countryside with his dog. His voice speaks over the scene, relating the pageantry awaiting Roman conquerors returning home to great fanfare. He describes a frenzied scene where the conqueror basks in the adulation of the empire, but, behind the conqueror all the while, was a single slave whispering in his ear, "All glory is fleeting."

Fleeting is an apt description of the lifespan of all earthly achievements. Certainly achievements are neither forbidden nor frowned upon; however, we should always bear in mind they and the satisfaction we derive from them are fleeting.

My friend and fellow author Steve Van Winkle told about how his son has won his share of track and field events. Altogether, his high school medals probably weigh five pounds. "We celebrated all of those achievements with him and still remember the excitement of each meet. However, when he is in his upper thirties and trying to raise a family while pleasing a demanding boss, the glory of his track achievements will no longer satisfy him."

*The lesson is the satisfaction derived from even laudable earthly achievements will inevitably fade.*

That doesn't mean those achievements were worthless or unworthy of effort. The lesson to take is what everyone must learn and bear in mind over the years: the satisfaction derived from even laudable earthly achievements will inevitably fade.

Mastering this truth helps keeps our ambition from becoming ruthless and cutthroat while pursuing earthly achievements. Why? Because we understand exchanging something eternal like relationships and influence for anything fleeting leaves us diminished in the end. This type of fool's trade might best be illustrated in one of Jimmy Johnson's first reactions to being named head coach of the Dallas Cowboys.

After decades of coaching in the college ranks where he achieved the pinnacle of success in 1987 by winning the National Championship at the University of Miami, Johnson's ambition still dreamt of the day he would have the opportunity to achieve the ultimate football prize: winning a Super Bowl. His chance arrived in 1989 at the expense of a living legend.

The Cowboys had recently been purchased by Jerry Jones, a man of considerable ambition, achievement, and ego himself. As one of his first acts, Jones unceremoniously fired Hall of Fame coach Tom Landry, who had led the Cowboys since their inception in 1960.

His treatment of Landry was universally perceived as brutal, classless, and, worst of all, thankless. These were of little concern to Jones. He had ambitions for his new team and felt retaining the old coach wasn't compatible with the goal of winning championships, so he had to go.

Jones, however, knew a man of similar ambitions as himself who was perfectly suited for the task at hand. Tapped by his old schoolmate as the new head coach of the Cowboys, Jimmy Johnson's chance at a Super Bowl had finally arrived.

To optimize the likelihood of achieving a Super Bowl victory, Coach Johnson took a page from Jones's "How to Dump Significant People Playbook" and determined he could not be both married and also fully pursue football glory. His twenty-six year marriage and his ambitions were incompatible. A simple choice remained.

After taking his wife to dinner, Johnson sat her down and told her he could either be head football coach of the Dallas Cowboys or married. And he'd decided to be head football coach of the Dallas Cowboys.

During his time as coach of the Cowboys, Johnson would win not one but two Super Bowls.

Along the way, however, his ambition wouldn't suffer him to do the hard work of balancing marriage and career goals. Instead, he utilized a shortcut that callously dismantled relationships within his own family by selfishly ending his twenty-six year marriage in hopes of achieving something that is, at best, fleeting.

In the kind of cruel twist the flesh enjoys inflicting on people, both Johnson's and owner Jerry Jones's ambitions and egos frequently collided until they determined they could no longer work together. Their parting of ways was announced only two months after Coach Johnson won his second consecutive Super Bowl with the Cowboys in 1993.

In the end, Jimmy Johnson inflicted upon his family the consequences of ending a marriage that lasted over a quarter-century so he could coach the Dallas Cowboys for five years. Then, like Tom Landry before him, Johnson was unceremoniously ushered out of his position; he never again coached in a Super Bowl.

Though impressive, gentleness would have discerned the actual value of winning a Super Bowl. Gentleness would have recognized Johnson was exchanging something of eternal value for something that would fade and wouldn't have allowed him to even consider the choice he made between his wife and his ambition.

Compare these men of naked ambition to Jesus when an angry mob cast a woman caught in adultery at His feet demanding an answer on whether she should be punished as the law required. Jesus could have looked at the crowd and seen the advantage of pleasing the many over tending the one who had nothing to offer Him. He could simply have affirmed the law that demanded she be executed and immediately alleviated Himself of the pressure.

Jesus, however, spoke gently to her. She, and the treatment of her that the mob would witness and would be recorded in Scripture, mattered in eternity. He cared more about the woman lying helplessly on the ground than elevating His stature with the group of vigilantes demanding justice. (See John 8:1–12.) What would have happened if Jesus had been someone of ambition and more concerned about personal achievement than gently considering one woman who was in peril of dying alone?

> *Jesus cared more about the woman lying helplessly on the ground than elevating His stature with the group of vigilantes demanding justice.*

This is the superiority of gentleness as a satisfying means to the hunger for achievement. While we understand earthly achievements will ultimately fade, we may still pursue and realize them. But in doing so, we'll find ourselves considering others, placing their well being ahead of our ambition and refusing to treat them as expendable.

In short, gentleness refuses to pursue earthly achievements at the expense of others and eternity.

## THE PRIORITY OF HOW

In addition to discerning the actual value of an earthly achievement, we must prioritize the how when pursuing eternal ones.

> *Gentleness refuses to pursue earthly achievements at the expense of others and eternity.*

Gentleness is an absolute necessity when pursuing eternal achievements because the means by which we pursue them determines if we achieve them at all. Eternal achievements make the how a nonnegotiable priority, whereas the flesh rarely concerns itself with how earthly achievements are realized: the importance is the achievement.

For example, Jimmy Johnson was just as celebrated for winning a Super Bowl after abandoning his wife as he would have been had he have never made his prior unseemly choice. Likewise, in light of revelations Henry Murray was conducting unethical experiments for the CIA, his name has not been withdrawn as a recipient of the Gold Medal Award of the American Psychological Association.

Society and the flesh are typically more concerned with the achievements themselves than the means employed to realize them.

However, eternal achievements must be pursued in a way compatible with the Spirit and with Scripture. In other words, no one will achieve greatness in the kingdom who pursues it while ignoring the needs of others, and no one will achieve first place in the kingdom who refuses to humble themselves and put others before them.

The *how* is the priority; *how we pursue eternal achievements determines if we achieve them.* Understanding this truth keeps ambition safely away from envy and prevents selfish ambition from forming because we know those kinds of ambition can never achieve eternal goals.

While the fleshly shortcuts to achievement of envy and murder seem efficient and effective, they always victimize people in the process. Gentleness, on the other hand, is the Spirit's counterintuitive means to achievement that is at once powerful and effective while valuing the people in our lives above all.

Back in the New Testament, James immediately followed his observation about every evil work being found where selfish ambition lives by reminding his readers that, in contrast, the "wisdom that is from above" is marked by gentleness (James 3:17).

His words clarify our choices for pursuing achievement. We can either allow the evil means of envious, selfish ambition to brutalize people as we strive toward our goals or we can honor God's wisdom and pursue achievement through gentleness . . . and thereby ensuring our ambitions never injure anyone in our lives.

What utterly satisfies our hunger for achievement (our N-Ach) is not the achievements themselves but knowing they have been pursued according to gentleness.

> *Eternal achievements must be pursued in a way compatible with the Spirit and with Scripture.*

> *How we pursue eternal achievements determines if we achieve them.*

ENVY/MURDERS → ACHIEVEMENT ← GENTLENESS

# CHAPTER 10

# THE HUNGER
# FOR PLEASURE

W hen I first arrived at Bible college, a professor stood on the first day of classes and asked everyone in the class of freshmen to turn to the Book of Hezekiah in the Old Testament. Naturally, at this request most people grabbed their Bibles and began thumbing dutifully through Scripture looking for Hezekiah.

Pages turned and the minutes went by until one-by-one all the faces in the room began looking at one another and eventually up toward the professor. He was looking back at us wondering how long it would take for everyone to give up the futile search.

There is no such Book of Hezekiah in the Old Testament, or any other Testament for that matter. However, it sounds like it should be there, doesn't it?

The search for it is actually an old Bible college initiation designed to help newcomers understand that, no matter how much they went to church or how much they had prepared for the first day of school, there was a lot to learn. The first lesson is that not everything that sounds biblical is.

*Not everything that sounds biblical is.*

They are any number of common clichés that fit this profile; they can be categorized in several ways.

First are the quotations commonly believed to originate in the Bible but are completely absent from its pages. "God helps those who help themselves" is one such quote; not only is this quote nowhere to be found in the Bible, it is actually completely contradictory to the message of God in Scripture. God is emphatic: We cannot help ourselves, and God helps those who actually embrace *this* truth.

There are summations of biblical ideas couched in ways the Bible never uses. "Spare the rod and spoil the child" is an example of such. Certainly the Bible has much to say about raising kids, and it even uses the words *spare* and *rod* in connection with it.

Then, there are biblical-sounding phrases that just miss what the Scripture teaches. The reason they miss is because in quoting a verse, the accuracy is only about ninety-nine percent of the verse. But omission of the one percent actually changes everything about what the verse teaches. For example, "Money is the root of all evil," sounds especially biblical since Jesus and the disciples weren't motoring around Palestine in Rolls Royces, and who hasn't seen money at the center of broken friendships and families?

Because of this Bible-sounding proverb, however, we also face questions from skeptics. Money is the root of all evil? Money . . . all evil? Money was at the root of Hitler's Reich? Money was the reason for political prisoners exiled in Soviet Russia? Serial killers and abusers are sourced in money?

Soon, it becomes impossible to defend this statement not only because we really can't trace *all* evil back to money but also because we must have money to live. Families are often glad to help loved ones who need some assistance in opening a business or just getting through the month; will this doom the family? Probably not! This cliché is an incomplete version of 1 Timothy 6:10, and perhaps it sounds so biblical because it is lifted *nearly* verbatim from Scripture. The problem is a couple key omissions.

First Timothy records the aging Apostle Paul's instruction to young Timothy for leading a church and understanding ministry. In the full text of the verse, Paul warns his young protégé, "The love of money is a root of all kinds of evils" (ESV).

When seen in its entirety, the verse is obviously not teaching that money itself is the root of all evil in the world but rather that the love of money is at the root of a host of evil things. Even though the cliché is popular and Bible sounding, it is a complete misrepresentation of what Scripture actually teaches.

This is also a common problem when it comes to pleasure and Scripture. Much like the statements above, which are either wrong or wrongly attributed to the Bible (or both), some people perceive the Bible as condemning pleasure of any kind.

It's hard to say when this perception took hold on society. It is nothing new. It likely goes back further than we have records to prove. But we know the Stoics—whose founder lived during the third century—believed we should abstain from worldly pleasure, and a few centuries ago a very old sect of Christians known as Puritans propagated the same. They were very concerned about their namesake, a form of the word *purity*. Their reputation is so ingrained in American society that as late as the early twentieth century, H. L. Mencken, famous and acerbic writer for *The Baltimore Sun* newspaper, defined Puritanism as "the haunting fear that someone, somewhere may be happy."[35] Another even more contemporary satirist, Garrison Keillor, commented that the Puritans landed in America "in 1648 in the hope of finding greater restrictions than were permissible under English law at that time."

This chapter's hunger is not about the Stoics or the Puritans, but it is concerned with pleasure, something about which some people believe the Bible is ardently opposed. Properly or not, when it comes to anything pleasing or touching the fringe of enjoyment, the reputation of Christianity has developed in a way that makes people think such things must be appropriated in spite of it.

This notion highlights why Paul uses a couple terms for the counterfeit methods to pleasure that are perhaps the most prevalent in our culture today. When people begin to believe that enjoyments are frowned upon, the means by which they procure them are usually illicit as well; after all, if what we seek is "banned," what difference does it make how we acquire it?

The fact is, everyone hungers for pleasure in their lives. No matter what we believe, regardless of our backgrounds, and even in spite of our best efforts, the hunger for pleasure remains.

The French mathematician and theologian, Blaise Pascal wrote, "All men seek happiness without exception. They all aim at this goal however different the means they use to attain it."

Pascal's observation aptly describes this universal hunger for pleasure. We all seek it; we all desire it. And, eventually, we *will* all pursue it whether we feel it is permissible or not. That's the power of this hunger.

Sadly, for those who understand pleasure as an affront to God's will, the first result of this supposed forbidden desire is scorching guilt. When pleasure is perceived to be off-limits, people tend to feel that if they are good enough or holy enough or interested in the so-called nobler things of God, this desire will vanish.

---

35. Dave Rosenthal, "Happy birthday, H. L. Mencken," *The Baltimore Sun*, September 12, 2012, https://www.baltimoresun.com/bal-happy-birthday-hl-mencken-20120912-story.html.

When it doesn't, when it instead intensifies, guilt is added to the mix. Guilt, in this case, is illegitimate because God Himself has given us the hunger.

Pastor Kevin DeYoung, in an article for The Gospel Coalition, observes this about Christians in the church he pastors: "I'm convinced most serious Christians live their lives with an almost constant low-level sense of guilt." He continues and notes that this guilt, left unchecked, "can have a cumulative effect whereby even the mature Christian can feel like he's rather disappointing to God, maybe just barely Christian."[36]

Far from being a deterrent to pursuing pleasure, this type of illegitimate guilt only suppresses it; indeed, over time, this guilt's cumulative effect of suppressing this hunger actually begins to compress it until it explodes.

Often, that explosion takes the form of raw determination to experience the pleasure believed to be forbidden. And, while God has never forbidden pleasure, believing it is and determining to acquire it represents a dangerous place for anyone, because once a person decides to pursue a forbidden end, the means no longer matter.

Think of it like this: If someone decides to murder another, is that person concerned with laws against breaking and entering homes? Are they concerned about legally obtaining a weapon? In any way, do they experience a moral dilemma about stealing ammunition from a store?

Probably not! If the end they're pursuing is illegal, the legality of the means to that end are of no real consequence.

This is what's especially troubling about people who believe God does not want them to experience the pleasure they hunger for: Once the hunger becomes acute, the means to experiencing it no longer matter.

## MEANS MATTER

The flesh is happy to accommodate this misperception and the expedience it births. As always, it readily holds out counterfeit means to satisfy our hunger for pleasure. However, unlike no other hunger, seeking to satisfy this one with the deeds of the flesh guarantees sorrow not only in lives in the immediate vicinity but in generations to come.

When Paul takes this up in his letter to the Galatians, he lists two different means by which many people seek to assuage their hunger for pleasure. Both of them are toxic in unique ways.

---

36. Kevin DeYoung, "Are Christians Meant to Feel Guilty All the Time?" The Gospel Coalition, May 11, 2010, https://www.thegospelcoalition.org/blogs/kevin-deyoung/are-christians-meant-to-feel-guilty-all-the-time/.

He first mentions drunkenness. There can be little argument that alcohol in itself serves to produce a pleasurable sensation. After all, if this were not the case, its use would have faded out centuries ago.

Also of interest is the fact that the Greek word for drunkenness in this passage means "intoxication." John Constable, former professor at Dallas Theological Seminary, defines the word as meaning, "Excessive use of intoxicants."[37]

Paul is highlighting something that intoxicates, and this need not necessarily be alcohol. Any substance that significantly alters our brain function can be classified as an intoxicant.

Did you know alcohol affects the same areas of the brain as Valium and other depressants? Any type of psychotropic drug would be linked to this passage as a counterfeit means of experiencing pleasure.

Intoxicants themselves offer instant pleasure for a variety of people. When using them, people are able to disengage from responsibilities and let go. This is a common use when people are swept up in a strict daily routine or lifestyle. Not only do intoxicants allow people who are normally staid and disciplined to unwind from the tension of their routine, but it can also dull the sensation of pain or loss generated by tragedy or even feelings of sorrow aroused from daily reports of treachery and injustice.

For any of these maladies, there stands ready any number of remedies in pill, bottle, inhalant, or a variety of other forms to release our minds from considering one more unpleasantry. And, while we know the release is only temporary, many reach for these substances because they offer quick escape that requires neither discipline nor preparation on our part.

What also needs to be remembered at this point is that Paul is not speaking of ends here. He is listing means to ends. While intoxicants can certainly be both, perhaps the more prevalent use of their power to help us realize pleasure is found in the second term Paul uses: revelries.

*Revelries* is a word not in use much anymore, but it has a particular application as a counterfeit means to pleasure. The word Paul uses could also be translated "carousal" and expands on the use of intoxicants. Constable defines it as "parties involving excessive eating and drinking."

When anyone hungers for pleasure, a usual requirement is other people. Whether it be for laughter or sexual gratification, or even the pleasure some derive from expressing anger, other people are essential. Yet no matter the type

---

37. John Constable, "Expository Notes of Dr. Thomas Constable: Galatians 5," Bible Commentaries, StudyLight.org, accessed March 6, 2019, https://www.studylight.org/commentaries/dcc/galatians-5.html.

of pleasure chased, and no matter how many people surround us, good sense usually captures any attempt at reckless pleasure seeking and dismantles it before we have a chance to do something regrettable.

This is why the word *revelries* is important to understand. It combines the two essentials needed to provide a variety of instant pleasures: intoxicants and people.

Let the hunger for pleasure seethe long enough, and eventually satisfying it will seem urgent, bordering on a crisis. And when people are desperate for this satisfaction, they often find themselves at parties where intoxicants are used excessively.

Why are inhibitions lowered when people drink alcohol? In an article for *Psychology Today* psychologist Dr. Joshua Gowin explains alcohol is more than a depressant, as had been traditionally thought; it also elevates levels of norepinephrine, which in turn increases impulsivity. He went on to say, "Drunken brains are primed to seek pleasure without considering the consequences; no wonder so many hook-ups happen after happy hour."

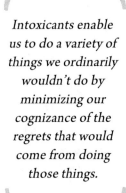

*Intoxicants enable us to do a variety of things we ordinarily wouldn't do by minimizing our cognizance of the regrets that would come from doing those things.*

The research further showed that alcohol, while increasing levels of norepinephrine, actually lowered activity in the prefrontal and temporal cortex of the brain, the regions responsible for decision-making and rational thought. According to the article, this lowered brain activity "further explains why alcohol causes us to act without thinking. The prefrontal cortex also plays a role in preventing aggressive behavior, so this might help explain the relationship between alcohol and violence."[38]

What alcohol and other intoxicants do is reduce our inhibitions and capacities for making sound decisions. Both of these effects are useful in the pursuit of immediate, fleshly pleasure. The reason alcohol has been called liquid courage can also be applied to all intoxicants: They enable us to do a variety of things we ordinarily wouldn't do by minimizing our cognizance of the regrets that would come from doing those things.

---

38. Joshua Gowin, "Your Brain on Alcohol," *Psychology Today,* June 18, 2010, https://www.psychologytoday .com/us/blog/you-illuminated/201006/your-brain-alcohol.

This is what happens when people starve themselves of pleasure, especially when they believe they are doing so in the name of God. This hunger will only pressurize until it finds a release in either drunkenness or revelries.

## AT HIS RIGHT HAND

These regrets have flowered in our society at alarming levels. It's created a narcissistic culture that pursues whatever makes us happy regardless of the resulting forms of behavior.

This is the breakdown that occurs when people believe pleasure is something God frowns upon and demands people abstain from. Indeed, as we have discussed, when that idea is embraced, we essentially suppress this hunger until the only way to pursue it is pragmatic and offensive to God.

The alternative to this is what Paul calls *temperance*. Before exploring this word, however, let's clarify something: the Bible encourages pleasure.

Certainly there are some pleasures placed off limits from people, but the general idea of pleasure and even seeking it is nowhere prohibited in even a sentence contained in the Bible. A quick scan of a handful of verses demonstrates this.

First Timothy 6:17 says God "gives us richly all things to enjoy" while James 1:17 reminds us, "Every good and perfect gift is from above."

Still, Psalm 16:11 is the definitive verse regarding pleasures. David writes, "You will show me the path of life; in Your presence is fullness of joy; at Your right hand there are pleasures forevermore."

David is obviously speaking about life and its progression through time and, on this path, he declares the joy and pleasure we seek are indeed available; in fact, he says joy to the full and everlasting pleasures are found in God's presence.

That's a very strange declaration if God is against our pursuit of pleasure. What isn't as easy to discern, however, is that if the pleasures we seek are at God's right hand, then the means by which we realize them are much, much different from the counterfeit ones held out by the flesh.

This is why Paul uses the word *temperance*. The word refers to moderation or self-control and reminds us again that every good pleasure we seek is only available if it is pursued properly.

Ben Johnson was born in Jamaica and immigrated with his parents to Canada when he was a teen. Johnson was a natural runner and teamed up with running coach Charlie Francis soon after arriving in his new country.

Johnson trained at York University and found his first international recognition as a sprinter in Brisbane, Australia, where he won two silver medals at the Commonwealth Games six years after arriving in Canada; this would soon propel him to the Olympic Games.

In the 1984 Olympics in Los Angeles, Ben Johnson reached the finals of the one hundred-meter sprint, taking a bronze medal in the event. He finished behind an American sprinter named Carl Lewis. Lewis became Johnson's archrival, and their competition for fastest man in the world routinely made headlines in all major newspapers.

Johnson set a new one hundred-meter world record in 1987 of 9.83 seconds, beating the previous record by a full tenth of a second. A full tenth of a second wasn't just setting a new world record; Johnson destroyed the old one. A year later, Johnson took gold at the 1988 Olympics in Seoul, and he did so by besting his own world record by .04 seconds.

However, a cloud began to form over his accomplishments when he tested positive for steroids. It took the Olympic Committee only three days to disqualify Johnson; his gold medal was subsequently awarded to the second place finisher, Carl Lewis.

Not only was Johnson stripped of his medal, his world records from both the World Championships in 1987 and the 1988 Olympics were rescinded when he admitted using steroids in both contests. Ben Johnson was suspended from competition and wouldn't race again for three years.

When Johnson used steroids as a shortcut to success, he won races and set records and claimed medals. However, when the shortcut was discovered, he lost everything.

*At its root, temperance means self-mastery; it means not being subject to whim or driven of our own desires.*

This is what happens when people choose the counterfeit shortcuts of the flesh. They will win, they will find pleasure, but it will eventually be stripped from them because it is inherently shallow and superficial. This type of pleasure gives birth to regrets of all kinds.

Paul reminded his protégé, Timothy, "Also if anyone competes in athletics, he is not crowned unless he competes according to the rules" (2 Timothy 2:5). What the apostle is saying is that even if someone comes in first, he is not the winner unless he has competed lawfully, unless he has taken no shortcuts.

Temperance is the fruit of the Spirit that leads to genuine, lasting pleasure. For most, temperance is the last thing in the world they would suspect could satisfy such a deep hunger.

At its root, temperance means self-mastery; it means not being subject to whim or driven of our own desires. Understanding why temperance is the Spirit's path to pleasure lies in understanding that biblical pleasure is secured not only by different means but has at its heart a different end as well.

## A BETTER MEANS

We've spent considerable time excising the notion that the Bible is not opposed to pleasure; however, that is not to say all pleasure is biblical. In addition to that which is birthed from intentionally shortcutting the process, there is pleasure that is impetuous and carries consequences with it.

Perhaps one of the best examples of this is family. As a pastor, I've seen marriage and family life from all sides and in all conditions; it can be a strange experience.

Frequently, pastors are one of the first people to be informed of a young couple's intention to spend their lives together. Smiles fill the room as they talk about their future and what will come of it, and, mostly, they cannot wait to enter into this new phase of life.

*The Bible is not opposed to pleasure; however, that is not to say all pleasure is biblical.*

Weeks are then spent counseling the happy couple. This allows all scenarios to be laid out and discussed openly. Hopes, expectations, plans, pasts, and futures are all plotted in the safety of an office. The hope being that the little time spent together before the wedding will help forge a lifetime of blessings for the two in love and for the generations coming after them.

When the time comes to discuss difficult things, I don't suppose anyone I've ever spoken with has ever truly grasped the diary of dangers confronting marriage. Typically, when asked why they will not end up divorced like the other fifty percent of couples in America, there is a long list of commitments, dedications, and convictions they counter with that will insulate them from tragedy. Ultimately, most say they don't believe in divorce and it will never be an option.

"No one ever gets married with the intention of divorcing," I say, "and the vast majority of people who are divorced today said divorce was not an option before they married."

*Temperance has mastered moments and brought them into submission to better things.*

This usually causes an obvious introspection from the happy couple.

And it's a valuable introspection because in the many times I've had to keep a marriage from ending instead of beginning, the issues threatening the union arose impetuously.

I don't think anyone has ever planned to break trust, but it's shattered when in a moment someone decides to violate their vows. The moment of pleasure presents itself and someone seizes it. The number of times I've heard it called a "moment of weakness" is staggering.

Whether a moment or not, it was certainly weakness. The weakness was that the person guilty of sacrificing their family didn't take control of their urges or their shallow selfishness of desire and allowed himself or herself a "moment" of indulgence.

It is the opposite of temperance, which has mastered moments and brought them into submission to better things. Those who master self, master moments. Moments are the things from which lasting pleasure is built or sacrificed. There's really no in-between.

Temperance assures that we don't seek pleasure from a substance and then get behind the wheel of a car eventually shattering lives. It keeps us from justifying a lie that dismantles the esteem our kids have for us. Self-mastery disallows the weakness we all feel in certain moments that might grant pleasure in that moment but invariably lead to lifetimes of regret.

## BETTER ENDS

Once this fruit of the Spirit takes hold, we also become keenly aware that the Bible advocates for nobler pleasures. Nobler in that they aren't fleeting or capable of causing remorse.

Scripture often calls people to wait for what's better, sometimes even at the expense of pleasure for a moment. Moses's life is such an example.

Cast upon the Nile River by his own mother in order to save him from Pharaoh's evil decree to kill all the newborn Jewish males, Moses miraculously landed in the arms of Pharaoh's daughter instead of being swallowed by the dangers of the waters. This ironic twist meant that the very person Pharaoh sought to murder was raised under his own roof.

Moses enjoyed the luxuries and opulence of a king's grandson. No desire was off-limits; no pleasure was out-of-bounds. The world itself was at Moses's beck and call.

When the day came when Moses discovered he was actually Jewish, he decided to renounce his status in the lineage of Pharaoh and cast himself with the persecuted and tormented Israelites who were slaves in the empire. Moses traded in a lifetime of pleasure for a lifetime of pain and servile labor.

Scripture explains why, however, and it relates directly to the hunger we're considering. In the Book of Hebrews the writer says, "By faith Moses, when he was grown up, refused to be called the son of Pharaoh's daughter, choosing rather to be mistreated with the people of God than to enjoy the fleeting pleasures of sin. He considered the reproach of Christ greater wealth than the treasures of Egypt, for he was looking to the reward" (Hebrews 11:24–26 ESV).

When you look closely at the passage, several things stand out; but of all of them, one that cannot be missed is that Moses refused to trade deep, lasting pleasure offered by God for the immediate, varied pleasures available only to royalty. The reason is simple: the pleasures in Pharaoh's house were fleeting, and Moses was looking to the reward God offered.

What isn't so apparent is that God's reward was not immediate like Pharaoh's. To receive the lasting, satisfying pleasure God offered, Moses had to spurn the opulence of pleasure available immediately. The only way he was able to do this was through exercising temperance.

What Moses embodies here is also evident in Christ's words to those who hunger for pleasure and are tempted to settle for the saccharine substitute offered by the flesh. In Matthew 16, Jesus asked a question that has hung over creation for two thousand years: "For what will it profit a man if he gains the whole world and forfeits his soul? Or what shall a man give in return for his soul?" (Matthew 16:26 ESV).

It's the question Moses confronted. What if everything in the world was suddenly yours for all your life, but to get it, you had to surrender your eternal soul? Is it a good bargain? Is it something acceptable to agree to, even in a moment of weakness?

Temperance demands that, whatever we might stand to gain in this life, in this moment we call life, it is not a fair trade for the pleasure we could have for eternity. "Hold out for the eternal!" is what temperance would counsel, because instead of enjoyable pleasures for a few decades, we could rather have full joy and pleasures for eternity. Temperance is able to see the superiority of the eternal over the fleeting.

This shouldn't be construed as meaning the only pleasure temperance allows is in the hereafter; nothing is further from the truth.

Go back to our happy couple longing to be married. Visualize their wedding day, bright and beautiful. Watch as they bring their first and their second child home; rejoice as careers are advanced and dreams are realized. Then, be concerned as the arguments come. Worry as unspoken frustrations mount and selfishness finds cracks in their relationship.

And go with one of them as they are out of town at a conference. Watch temptation present itself and pleasure cast itself in their lap.

*The Spirit holds out temperance for genuine pleasure seekers because seekers of genuine pleasure understand the only pleasure that is genuine is one that is noble and eternal.*

If this pleasure is spurned, will the payoff only come in the afterlife? No. If temperance is heeded, not only will this fleeting pleasure be rejected, but also other better, deeper pleasures will rise in its place. Pleasures like the untainted love of kids, kids who don't have to take sides with their parents. Pleasures like growing old together instead of splitting a home or living with a lifetime of mistrust. Pleasures like Christmases united as a family instead of trading off holidays.

The Spirit holds out temperance for genuine pleasure seekers because seekers of genuine pleasure understand the only pleasure that is genuine is one that is noble and eternal. They know this because temperance guides them through the often-choppy waters of temptations and decisions to lead them to satisfy their hunger for pleasure meaningfully.

DRUNKENNESS/REVELRIES → PLEASURE ← TEMPERANCE

# CHAPTER 11

# IN SEARCH
# FOR YOUR SOUL HUNGER

Y ou've probably heard someone say pain and pleasure are the two
motivations that drive us to action. We mostly all know this seems
true. These two motivators steer us to where we want to go or away
from what we know will hurt us. If there is enough pain, we will turn every stone
to find a solution to alleviate it. If there is the want for a particular pleasure, we
will seek in every nook and cranny or maneuver every circumstantial barrier
that blocks our path to that pleasure.

Life skills coach Adam Sicinski says in his blog post, "How to Use the Pain
and Pleasure Principle to Achieve a Goal," "The pain-pleasure principle lies at
the core of everything you do, and of everything you are. Your beliefs, values
and psychological rules are all built upon this principle."[39]

Despite this common thinking, I've written the first ten chapters of this book
to discourage such thinking. The driving force of the five senses is not what they
feel in the context of pain or pleasure but how they react to the God-given hungers given us at creation. Although we are a creation observing the world
through the five senses, which makes us sensual creatures, our beliefs and values
cannot be solely based on those five components. Even animals have these five
senses, and what we see, hear, touch, taste, or feel cannot always be trusted. All
of us have witnessed a master of sleight of hand and believed something that

---

39. Adam Sicinski, "How to Use the Pain and Pleasure Principle to Achieve a Goal," *IQ Matrix* (blog),
accessed November 29, 2018, https://blog.iqmatrix.com/pain-pleasure-principle.

was not true. Even though we knew it was a sleight of hand, our minds still wanted to believe it. We have all heard something from a credible source that turned out to be false. We have touched a synthetic fur that was not genuine, but it *felt* so real. And who hasn't picked up a scented candle and enjoyed the fragrance of a chocolate bar that if tasted would be waxy and bitter?

> *We know instinctively this life isn't all there is, and we hunger to find out more.*

And above all, these five temporal components of our being bow the knee to two powerful realities. One is survival. For if our fear for life and limb is triggered, then our need for survival trumps all five senses because survival is hardwired within us.

But we also have hardwired within us a concept of eternity. God set eternity into every person's heart (Ecclesiastes 3:11). Because of it, we know instinctively this life isn't all there is, and we hunger to find out more. Although we desire relationships with others and are well aware of our self-existence, what God has out there is beyond the sensual. It is spiritual, and it is eternal.

What Adam Sicinski wrote in his blog latently reveals that hungers do indeed exist, but his solutions lead us directly to the door of the works of the flesh. To assuage those hungers he suggests a behavioral modification he calls *pattern interrupt*.

> This "pattern interrupt" can come in the form of a specific set of words you say to yourself such as "Stop it, right now!"; it can be in the form of an "action" of beating your chest with your fist or simply spinning around in a circle for a few seconds. It can also be as simple as singing something to yourself or reading a quote that helps you stay focused on what's most important. Finally, it could come in the form of a question that snaps you out of your current state-of-mind. It really doesn't matter what it is. The purpose is that it breaks your pattern and immediately interrupts the behavior you are indulging in.[40]

*Pattern interrupt* is another way to avoid or make void the fruit of the Spirit. In other words, what it seems to be saying is engage in this action until your mind

---

40. Ibid.

adjusts to an acceptance mode, and then try it again. After all . . . where else is there to go?

## HUNGERS CHART

The fruit of the Spirit is found in Galatians 5:22–23. This is the gift God has available for us directly coming from His Holy Spirit. This fruit will satisfy the hungers He placed within us at creation. We know hungers are there because Jesus Himself in His famous Sermon on the Mount says to us, "Blessed are those who hunger and thirst for righteousness, for they shall be filled" (Matthew 5:6). So we are blessed when our appetites look toward the righteous. Then in His goodness He will offer that which will satisfy that hunger.

*The word* fruit *in the passage in Galatians is singular, meaning all nine are to be seen as a whole.*

The word *fruit* in the passage in Galatians is singular, meaning all nine are to be seen as a whole. All of these qualities will be demonstrated across the believer's life. In a perfect world there would be no need for substitutes for any of these traits. Thus walking in the Spirit would be a walk in the park. Similarly, our bodies are singular yet there are many parts that make up the whole. On any given day part of that whole can be out of sorts. The same can be true of our lives when attempting to partake of the fruit of the Spirit.

In the following chart, the fruit is listed in order within separate boxes, and the corresponding hungers as discussed in the previous chapters are arranged as well.

*Galatians 5:22–23*     **THE FRUIT OF THE SPIRIT**

| Love | Joy | Peace | Longsuffering | Kindness | Goodness | Faithfulness | Gentleness | Self-Control |
|------|-----|-------|---------------|----------|----------|--------------|------------|--------------|
| | | | **THE** | **HUMAN** | **HUNGER** | | | |
| Intimacy | Happiness | Contentment | Justice | Control | Respect | Truth | Achievement | Pleasure |
| | | | | | | | | |
| | | | | | | | | |

The next chart includes a breakdown of the three areas where the fruit of the Spirit affects our relationships: to God, others, and self. This breakdown is found in Luke 10:27, "'You shall love the LORD your God with all you heart, with all your soul, with all your strength, and with all your mind,' and 'your neighbor as yourself,'" and is further clarified in Ephesians 4:31–32, "Let all bitterness, wrath, anger, clamor, and evil speaking be put away from you, with all malice. And be kind to one another, tenderhearted, forgiving one another, even as God in Christ forgave you."

The first three components of the fruit go to your relationship to God. The second three concern your relationship to others, and the last three belong to your relationship to yourself. Take some time and acquaint yourself with these categories, also studying the corresponding hungers in context. If needed, go back to the parallel chapters to refresh your memory.

*Ephesians 4:31–32*

| RELATIONSHIP TO GOD | | | RELATIONSHIP TO OTHERS | | | RELATIONSHIP TO SELF | | |
|---|---|---|---|---|---|---|---|---|
| *Galatians 5:22–23* | | | THE FRUIT OF THE SPIRIT | | | | | |
| Love | Joy | Peace | Longsuffering | Kindness | Goodness | Faithfulness | Gentleness | Self-Control |
| Intimacy | Happiness | Contentment | THE JUSTICE | HUMAN Control | HUNGER Respect | Truth | Achievement | Pleasure |

Our next chart contains the antithesis of the fruit of the Spirit called the works of the flesh. It is no surprise how they correspond. Satan attempts to be as close to what God is doing while staying as far away from the truth as he can. He desires to create look-alikes. It is as though he is saying, "Okay, if You have produced something to draw their hunger toward righteousness, then I will produce an offer that which will draw them toward unrighteousness." That list can be found in Galatians 5:19–21. Now it should become clear what the common ground is where the Spirit wars against the flesh and the flesh wars against the Spirit.

*Ephesians 4:31–32*

| RELATIONSHIP TO GOD | | | RELATIONSHIP TO OTHERS | | | RELATIONSHIP TO SELF | | |
|---|---|---|---|---|---|---|---|---|

*Galatians 5:22–23* — THE FRUIT OF THE SPIRIT

| Love | Joy | Peace | Longsuffering | Kindness | Goodness | Faithfulness | Gentleness | Self-Control |
|---|---|---|---|---|---|---|---|---|
| | | | **THE** | **HUMAN** | **HUNGER** | | | |
| Intimacy | Happiness | Contentment | Justice | Control | Respect | Truth | Achievement | Pleasure |
| | | | | | | | | |
| Adultery Fornication | Uncleanness Licentiousness | Idolatry Sorcery | Hatred Contentions | Jealousies Anger | Selfish Ambitions Dissensions | Heresies ("My truth") | Envy Murder | Drunkenness Revelries |
| | | | | THE WORKS OF THE FLESH | | | | |

*Galatians 5:19–20*

In the following chart, the devil, of course, also has a breakdown of three areas where relationships are affected. These three components are found in 1 John 2:16, "For all that is in the world—the lust of the flesh, the lust of the eyes, and the pride of life—is not of the Father but is of the world." Notice every relationship is me, me, me!

*Ephesians 4:31–32*

| RELATIONSHIP TO GOD | | | RELATIONSHIP TO OTHERS | | | RELATIONSHIP TO SELF | | |
|---|---|---|---|---|---|---|---|---|

*Galatians 5:22–23* — THE FRUIT OF THE SPIRIT

| Love | Joy | Peace | Longsuffering | Kindness | Goodness | Faithfulness | Gentleness | Self-Control |
|---|---|---|---|---|---|---|---|---|
| | | | **THE** | **HUMAN** | **HUNGER** | | | |
| Intimacy | Happiness | Contentment | Justice | Control | Respect | Truth | Achievement | Pleasure |
| | | | | | | | | |
| Adultery Fornication | Uncleanness Licentiousness | Idolatry Sorcery | Hatred Contentions | Jealousies Anger | Selfish Ambitions Dissensions | Heresies ("My truth") | Envy Murder | Drunkenness Revelries |
| | | | | THE WORKS OF THE FLESH | | | | |

*Galatians 5:19–20*

| LUST OF THE FLESH—"ME" | | | LUST OF THE FLESH—"ME" | | | PRIDE OF LIFE—"ME" | | |
|---|---|---|---|---|---|---|---|---|

Next, our chart highlights how the beginning of every day offers us choices. Notice the up and down arrows. We can choose to ascend to the fruit of the

Spirit and thereby walk in the Spirit, or we have the choice to descend into the works of the flesh, thereby submitting to the surrogates. Jesus gives one of the most emotional invitations for a world weary of dealing with substitutes. He says, "Come to Me, all you who labor and are heavy laden, and I will give you rest" (Matthew 11:28). This chart represents the Joshua challenge: "Choose for yourselves this day whom you will serve" (Joshua 24:15).

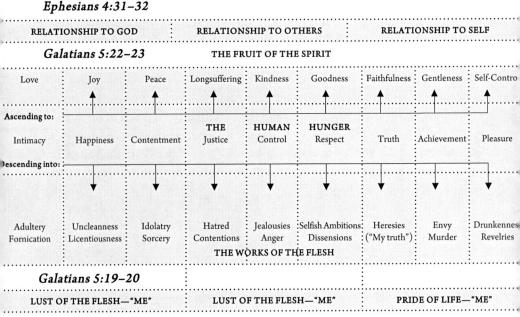

*Ephesians 4:31–32*

| RELATIONSHIP TO GOD | | | RELATIONSHIP TO OTHERS | | | RELATIONSHIP TO SELF | | |
|---|---|---|---|---|---|---|---|---|

*Galatians 5:22–23* — **THE FRUIT OF THE SPIRIT**

| Love | Joy | Peace | Longsuffering | Kindness | Goodness | Faithfulness | Gentleness | Self-Control |
|---|---|---|---|---|---|---|---|---|
| | | | ↑ THE | ↑ HUMAN | ↑ HUNGER | ↑ | ↑ | ↑ |
| Intimacy | Happiness | Contentment | Justice | Control | Respect | Truth | Achievement | Pleasure |
| ↓ | ↓ | ↓ | ↓ | ↓ | ↓ | ↓ | ↓ | ↓ |
| Adultery Fornication | Uncleanness Licentiousness | Idolatry Sorcery | Hatred Contentions | Jealousies Anger | Selfish Ambitions Dissensions | Heresies ("My truth") | Envy Murder | Drunkenness Revelries |

**THE WORKS OF THE FLESH**

*Galatians 5:19–20*

| LUST OF THE FLESH—"ME" | | LUST OF THE FLESH—"ME" | | PRIDE OF LIFE—"ME" | |
|---|---|---|---|---|---|

*1 John 2:15–16*

## LOOKING FOR MARKERS

If you want to see the grassroots of this country, there are highways crisscrossing the landscape of this great land that offer stunning scenes. Scenes you will miss, marvels never to be enjoyed, if you are sitting in an airplane. The fast pace of our society mandates a fly-over culture, and I understand that. Even so there are visual thrills to be enjoyed that for the flyer will remain unappreciated.

For the ten-year reunion of her graduation from college, my wife Gail and I decided to load into our two-seater Datsun 240Z car and head to Springfield, Missouri. Wait . . . I need to tell you we had two children with us. Matthew, our oldest, was seven, and our only daughter then, Rebecca, was five. I also need to tell you this was before seatbelt laws. They sat behind the two seats on a platform designed into that particular vehicle. Strut towers served as the back for their seats. They fit perfectly. When they tired of sitting, they would move the small amount of luggage around, lay on a pallet provided by mom that was spread on the carpeted platform that housed the spare tire, and sleep. It was cozy. It was fun.

We were young and adventurous, and poor. That meant we couldn't afford a hotel, so we planned to drive straight through from LA. We caught Interstate 40 at Barstow, California. Its asphalt follows the ups and downs, left and right bends and curves moving across America like a sea serpent all the way to Wilmington, North Carolina. But we were only going to Missouri. We saw America at its grassroots. One can't see what we saw from a plane.

By the time we were entering Amarillo, Texas, we were road weary. So I pulled into a 24/7 market a couple of hours past midnight and parked in what looked like a safe area. With the doors locked and the children long since sound asleep, Gail and I leaned our seats back and took a snooze. The off-and-on nocturnal customers didn't bother us, but at about 7:00 in the morning we were awakened by a series of knocks on the hood. It was a group of high schoolers looking through the windshield on their way to school. They were probably making sure we weren't dead!

We went inside to wash our faces and brush our teeth; we grabbed some coffee and orange juice and hit the road. Gail decided to drive. I quickly fell back asleep. I awakened to the fence posts zipping by us at an amazing rate. I leaned over slowly toward Gail and saw the speedometer at 115 miles per hour. She was in her own world humming a song without a care in the world. She had no idea of her speed, and I didn't want to startle her. "Uh-h, hon, how fast are you going?" She looked at her speedometer and immediately lifted her foot off of the pedal! Of course when she slowed to seventy miles per hour, it seemed as though we would never get there! (By the way, we still have that car. The gauge says it can do 160, but as far as I know, she wins the prize for speed in our family!).

I had no idea where we were except somewhere between Amarillo and Oklahoma City. I could see the road stretching out in front of us forever. We were in the zone where there were miles and miles of miles and miles. But along the edge of the road were little green signs every 5,280 feet. Each displayed a number that told me how far we were down the road. They helped me determine which direction we were going. And they of course help now, anywhere I choose to go. Beginning at the south state line on north-south routes they increase as I travel north. On east-west routes they begin on the western state border and increase as I travel east. Those numbers tell me how far I've traveled inside a state. They are critical location points for help in case of a breakdown or an accident. If I need help I can know exactly where I am.

Similarly, I have laid out a mile marker. It is an evaluation that will help you know exactly where you are at this moment in your journey. In the first ten chapters I identified and defined nine hungers that you will at some point on your journey seek to satisfy. Each time you take the evaluation, according to how far down life's road you have traveled, and according to your current circumstances, your numbers may fluctuate. I will illustrate that fact in the case studies portion of this chapter. There may be a time where you are disconnected for whatever reason; the hunger for intimacy may haunt you after a loss of a relationship through death or divorce. Or maybe through some unfortunate unfairness you are looking to feed the hunger for justice or truth. The evaluation will bare that fact out for you. Through the evaluation you can see the counterfeit the devil will throw out as bait to distract you from the real, the fruit of the Spirit that is God-given to satisfy the hunger identified in this unfortunate situation. It will give you the information needed to make the right choice. You may need to go back to reread that chapter and familiarize yourself with the revealed hunger. You may also turn to the appendix where I share corresponding Scripture to allow the power of God's Word to strengthen your resolve to walk in the Spirit. The evaluation is your mile marker. Use it, and if necessary, get with a friend or a counselor to help you remain in the groove of your walk in the Spirit.

When you take the evaluation, always remember to trust your initial impression and circle it first. If you think too long you may talk yourself out of the truth. Deception is one of Satan's most effective tools. Do not allow it to be used on you!

Here it is. Let's do this!

## HUNGER EVALUATION[41]

*For each of the following questions, find the column that includes the word or words matching your answer most closely. Circle the number for that column. Select only one number for each question.* You can also take the evaluation online and learn more about the hungers at www.hungertest.strikingly.com.

---

41. Questions inspired and adapted from David Powlison's X-ray Questions, found in his book *Seeing With New Eyes.*

## 1. Which number describes what you want most out of life?

| 1 | 2 | 3 | 4 | 5 | 6 | 7 | 8 | 9 |
|---|---|---|---|---|---|---|---|---|
| Intimacy | Excitement | Tranquility | Fairness | Power | Deference | Certainty | Determination | Desire |
| Closeness | Ecstasy | Satisfaction | Civility | Rules | Value | Accuracy | Motivation | Gratification |
| Relationship | Delight | Comfort | Reasonableness | Influence | Honor | Authenticity | Ambition | Craving |

## 2. Which number is most important to you in difficult situations?

| 1 | 2 | 3 | 4 | 5 | 6 | 7 | 8 | 9 |
|---|---|---|---|---|---|---|---|---|
| Intimacy | Excitement | Tranquility | Fairness | Power | Deference | Certainty | Determination | Desire |
| Closeness | Ecstasy | Satisfaction | Civility | Rules | Value | Accuracy | Motivation | Gratification |
| Relationship | Delight | Comfort | Reasonableness | Influence | Honor | Authenticity | Ambition | Craving |

## 3. Which number motivates you the most?

| 1 | 2 | 3 | 4 | 5 | 6 | 7 | 8 | 9 |
|---|---|---|---|---|---|---|---|---|
| Intimacy | Excitement | Tranquility | Fairness | Power | Deference | Certainty | Determination | Desire |
| Closeness | Ecstasy | Satisfaction | Civility | Rules | Value | Accuracy | Motivation | Gratification |
| Relationship | Delight | Comfort | Reasonableness | Influence | Honor | Authenticity | Ambition | Craving |

## 4. Which number do you think God would choose to define you in hard times?

| 1 | 2 | 3 | 4 | 5 | 6 | 7 | 8 | 9 |
|---|---|---|---|---|---|---|---|---|
| Intimacy | Excitement | Tranquility | Fairness | Power | Deference | Certainty | Determination | Desire |
| Closeness | Ecstasy | Satisfaction | Civility | Rules | Value | Accuracy | Motivation | Gratification |
| Relationship | Delight | Comfort | Reasonableness | Influence | Honor | Authenticity | Ambition | Craving |

## 5. Which number describes what you think about most?

| 1 | 2 | 3 | 4 | 5 | 6 | 7 | 8 | 9 |
|---|---|---|---|---|---|---|---|---|
| Intimacy | Excitement | Tranquility | Fairness | Power | Deference | Certainty | Determination | Desire |
| Closeness | Ecstasy | Satisfaction | Civility | Rules | Value | Accuracy | Motivation | Gratification |
| Relationship | Delight | Comfort | Reasonableness | Influence | Honor | Authenticity | Ambition | Craving |

## 6. Which number would be closest to what comes into your mind the first thing each morning?

| 1 | 2 | 3 | 4 | 5 | 6 | 7 | 8 | 9 |
|---|---|---|---|---|---|---|---|---|
| Intimacy Closeness Relationship | Excitement Ecstasy Delight | Tranquility Satisfaction Comfort | Fairness Civility Reasonableness | Power Rules Influence | Deference Value Honor | Certainty Accuracy Authenticity | Determination Motivation Ambition | Desire Gratification Craving |

## 7. Which number has the power to bring you the most pleasure?

| 1 | 2 | 3 | 4 | 5 | 6 | 7 | 8 | 9 |
|---|---|---|---|---|---|---|---|---|
| Intimacy Closeness Relationship | Excitement Ecstasy Delight | Tranquility Satisfaction Comfort | Fairness Civility Reasonableness | Power Rules Influence | Deference Value Honor | Certainty Accuracy Authenticity | Determination Motivation Ambition | Desire Gratification Craving |

## 8. Which number makes you sad?

| 1 | 2 | 3 | 4 | 5 | 6 | 7 | 8 | 9 |
|---|---|---|---|---|---|---|---|---|
| Intimacy Closeness Relationship | Excitement Ecstasy Delight | Tranquility Satisfaction Comfort | Fairness Civility Reasonableness | Power Rules Influence | Deference Value Honor | Certainty Accuracy Authenticity | Determination Motivation Ambition | Desire Gratification Craving |

## 9. Which number are you most attracted to?

| 1 | 2 | 3 | 4 | 5 | 6 | 7 | 8 | 9 |
|---|---|---|---|---|---|---|---|---|
| Intimacy Closeness Relationship | Excitement Ecstasy Delight | Tranquility Satisfaction Comfort | Fairness Civility Reasonableness | Power Rules Influence | Deference Value Honor | Certainty Accuracy Authenticity | Determination Motivation Ambition | Desire Gratification Craving |

## 10. Which number is most important to accomplishing your agenda?

| 1 | 2 | 3 | 4 | 5 | 6 | 7 | 8 | 9 |
|---|---|---|---|---|---|---|---|---|
| Intimacy Closeness Relationship | Excitement Ecstasy Delight | Tranquility Satisfaction Comfort | Fairness Civility Reasonableness | Power Rules Influence | Deference Value Honor | Certainty Accuracy Authenticity | Determination Motivation Ambition | Desire Gratification Craving |

## 11. Which number reveals what's truly in your heart?

| 1 | 2 | 3 | 4 | 5 | 6 | 7 | 8 | 9 |
|---|---|---|---|---|---|---|---|---|
| Intimacy Closeness Relationship | Excitement Ecstasy Delight | Tranquility Satisfaction Comfort | Fairness Civility Reasonableness | Power Rules Influence | Deference Value Honor | Certainty Accuracy Authenticity | Determination Motivation Ambition | Desire Gratification Craving |

## 12. Which number would help you accomplish what you think you're incapable of?

| 1 | 2 | 3 | 4 | 5 | 6 | 7 | 8 | 9 |
|---|---|---|---|---|---|---|---|---|
| Intimacy | Excitement | Tranquility | Fairness | Power | Deference | Certainty | Determination | Desire |
| Closeness | Ecstasy | Satisfaction | Civility | Rules | Value | Accuracy | Motivation | Gratification |
| Relationship | Delight | Comfort | Reasonable-ness | Influence | Honor | Authenticity | Ambition | Craving |

## 13. Which number would you say God knows dominates your life?

| 1 | 2 | 3 | 4 | 5 | 6 | 7 | 8 | 9 |
|---|---|---|---|---|---|---|---|---|
| Intimacy | Excitement | Tranquility | Fairness | Power | Deference | Certainty | Determination | Desire |
| Closeness | Ecstasy | Satisfaction | Civility | Rules | Value | Accuracy | Motivation | Gratification |
| Relationship | Delight | Comfort | Reasonable-ness | Influence | Honor | Authenticity | Ambition | Craving |

## 14. Which number would you choose to describe what goes on inside you during trials?

| 1 | 2 | 3 | 4 | 5 | 6 | 7 | 8 | 9 |
|---|---|---|---|---|---|---|---|---|
| Intimacy | Excitement | Tranquility | Fairness | Power | Deference | Certainty | Determination | Desire |
| Closeness | Ecstasy | Satisfaction | Civility | Rules | Value | Accuracy | Motivation | Gratification |
| Relationship | Delight | Comfort | Reasonable-ness | Influence | Honor | Authenticity | Ambition | Craving |

## 15. Which number has the potential to arouse temptation most inside you?

| 1 | 2 | 3 | 4 | 5 | 6 | 7 | 8 | 9 |
|---|---|---|---|---|---|---|---|---|
| Intimacy | Excitement | Tranquility | Fairness | Power | Deference | Certainty | Determination | Desire |
| Closeness | Ecstasy | Satisfaction | Civility | Rules | Value | Accuracy | Motivation | Gratification |
| Relationship | Delight | Comfort | Reasonable-ness | Influence | Honor | Authenticity | Ambition | Craving |

## 16. Which number describes what makes you tick?

| 1 | 2 | 3 | 4 | 5 | 6 | 7 | 8 | 9 |
|---|---|---|---|---|---|---|---|---|
| Intimacy | Excitement | Tranquility | Fairness | Power | Deference | Certainty | Determination | Desire |
| Closeness | Ecstasy | Satisfaction | Civility | Rules | Value | Accuracy | Motivation | Gratification |
| Relationship | Delight | Comfort | Reasonable-ness | Influence | Honor | Authenticity | Ambition | Craving |

## 17. Which number do you organize your life around?

| 1 | 2 | 3 | 4 | 5 | 6 | 7 | 8 | 9 |
|---|---|---|---|---|---|---|---|---|
| Intimacy | Excitement | Tranquility | Fairness | Power | Deference | Certainty | Determination | Desire |
| Closeness | Ecstasy | Satisfaction | Civility | Rules | Value | Accuracy | Motivation | Gratification |
| Relationship | Delight | Comfort | Reasonableness | Influence | Honor | Authenticity | Ambition | Craving |

## 18. Which number do you find the most refuge in?

| 1 | 2 | 3 | 4 | 5 | 6 | 7 | 8 | 9 |
|---|---|---|---|---|---|---|---|---|
| Intimacy | Excitement | Tranquility | Fairness | Power | Deference | Certainty | Determination | Desire |
| Closeness | Ecstasy | Satisfaction | Civility | Rules | Value | Accuracy | Motivation | Gratification |
| Relationship | Delight | Comfort | Reasonableness | Influence | Honor | Authenticity | Ambition | Craving |

## 19. Which number would you say defines the opinion others have of you?

| 1 | 2 | 3 | 4 | 5 | 6 | 7 | 8 | 9 |
|---|---|---|---|---|---|---|---|---|
| Intimacy | Excitement | Tranquility | Fairness | Power | Deference | Certainty | Determination | Desire |
| Closeness | Ecstasy | Satisfaction | Civility | Rules | Value | Accuracy | Motivation | Gratification |
| Relationship | Delight | Comfort | Reasonableness | Influence | Honor | Authenticity | Ambition | Craving |

## 20. Which number defines the weight of failure in your life?

| 1 | 2 | 3 | 4 | 5 | 6 | 7 | 8 | 9 |
|---|---|---|---|---|---|---|---|---|
| Intimacy | Excitement | Tranquility | Fairness | Power | Deference | Certainty | Determination | Desire |
| Closeness | Ecstasy | Satisfaction | Civility | Rules | Value | Accuracy | Motivation | Gratification |
| Relationship | Delight | Comfort | Reasonableness | Influence | Honor | Authenticity | Ambition | Craving |

## 21. Which number describes what you feel are your rights?

| 1 | 2 | 3 | 4 | 5 | 6 | 7 | 8 | 9 |
|---|---|---|---|---|---|---|---|---|
| Intimacy | Excitement | Tranquility | Fairness | Power | Deference | Certainty | Determination | Desire |
| Closeness | Ecstasy | Satisfaction | Civility | Rules | Value | Accuracy | Motivation | Gratification |
| Relationship | Delight | Comfort | Reasonableness | Influence | Honor | Authenticity | Ambition | Craving |

## 22. Which number makes you feel secure in yourself?

| 1 | 2 | 3 | 4 | 5 | 6 | 7 | 8 | 9 |
|---|---|---|---|---|---|---|---|---|
| Intimacy | Excitement | Tranquility | Fairness | Power | Deference | Certainty | Determination | Desire |
| Closeness | Ecstasy | Satisfaction | Civility | Rules | Value | Accuracy | Motivation | Gratification |
| Relationship | Delight | Comfort | Reasonableness | Influence | Honor | Authenticity | Ambition | Craving |

## 23. Which number do you think about most often?

| 1 | 2 | 3 | 4 | 5 | 6 | 7 | 8 | 9 |
|---|---|---|---|---|---|---|---|---|
| Intimacy | Excitement | Tranquility | Fairness | Power | Deference | Certainty | Determination | Desire |
| Closeness | Ecstasy | Satisfaction | Civility | Rules | Value | Accuracy | Motivation | Gratification |
| Relationship | Delight | Comfort | Reasonable-ness | Influence | Honor | Authenticity | Ambition | Craving |

## 24. Which number do you pray and ask God for?

| 1 | 2 | 3 | 4 | 5 | 6 | 7 | 8 | 9 |
|---|---|---|---|---|---|---|---|---|
| Intimacy | Excitement | Tranquility | Fairness | Power | Deference | Certainty | Determination | Desire |
| Closeness | Ecstasy | Satisfaction | Civility | Rules | Value | Accuracy | Motivation | Gratification |
| Relationship | Delight | Comfort | Reasonable-ness | Influence | Honor | Authenticity | Ambition | Craving |

## 25. Which number defines victory in your life?

| 1 | 2 | 3 | 4 | 5 | 6 | 7 | 8 | 9 |
|---|---|---|---|---|---|---|---|---|
| Intimacy | Excitement | Tranquility | Fairness | Power | Deference | Certainty | Determination | Desire |
| Closeness | Ecstasy | Satisfaction | Civility | Rules | Value | Accuracy | Motivation | Gratification |
| Relationship | Delight | Comfort | Reasonable-ness | Influence | Honor | Authenticity | Ambition | Craving |

## 26. Which number describes how you spend your time?

| 1 | 2 | 3 | 4 | 5 | 6 | 7 | 8 | 9 |
|---|---|---|---|---|---|---|---|---|
| Intimacy | Excitement | Tranquility | Fairness | Power | Deference | Certainty | Determination | Desire |
| Closeness | Ecstasy | Satisfaction | Civility | Rules | Value | Accuracy | Motivation | Gratification |
| Relationship | Delight | Comfort | Reasonable-ness | Influence | Honor | Authenticity | Ambition | Craving |

## 27. Which number defines your priorities?

| 1 | 2 | 3 | 4 | 5 | 6 | 7 | 8 | 9 |
|---|---|---|---|---|---|---|---|---|
| Intimacy | Excitement | Tranquility | Fairness | Power | Deference | Certainty | Determination | Desire |
| Closeness | Ecstasy | Satisfaction | Civility | Rules | Value | Accuracy | Motivation | Gratification |
| Relationship | Delight | Comfort | Reasonable-ness | Influence | Honor | Authenticity | Ambition | Craving |

Count the number of times you circled each number,
then record the totals here:

| 1 | 2 | 3 | 4 | 5 | 6 | 7 | 8 | 9 |
|---|---|---|---|---|---|---|---|---|
| | | | | | | | | |

Don't be discouraged if you score an unusually high number on one component or if a zero lies on the blank. You are on a journey. The numbers will likely change in a couple of months, especially when you get victory over a struggle or gain control of a bad situation. This evaluation is designed to help you know where you are now. With this knowledge, those close to you and those you trust can know where you are and help you to heal and gain victory over the flesh.

## BARRY'S STORY

I was sitting at home in my living room when my cell phone rang . . . it was Barry. He is an impressive man. He spent his life building a large church, and not many of his peers are more respected than he. Barry and his wife have done an exceptional job raising their five children.

All seemed right in their life when all went wrong. Out of the blue, it appeared, Barry's lifelong love let him know she was leaving him. When the phone rang, I was ready for a fun conversation but was blindsided by that news. As I was trying to process what I had just heard, another call was trying to get through to my cell.

I looked at my phone screen.

It was Barry's wife.

I called her back after Barry and I hung up. She was adamant. There was no changing her mind. She said she had been living with a very angry man for forty years, and she just was not going to take it any longer.

Indeed, she walked out. Gail and I were heartsick.

I tried to get my mind around the anger statement. We had been on many trips with this couple, even cruises, and never witnessed that anger. So I asked Barry if he would take the hunger evaluation. I was hoping to see how intensely he was feeding any hunger for control.

When I got the results his score registered zero on the fifth hunger. There was no anger issue that emerged from his answers; his wife's filter for what constituted anger was off, but what did emerge told the story.

I will let him tell it in his own words:

> *Sometimes it is difficult to establish what you need to do to fix a problem when the problem goes undiagnosed. It is possible to exist in an unknowing state for years without anyone getting to the heart of the problem or even to dismiss anyone who tries to discuss the need with you as either unknowing or just plain insignificant. This is especially*

*true if you lead a large number of people and they look to you as their leader. It is said that absolute power corrupts absolutely, and I find that statement to be true.*

*Although I wasn't a tyrant, I was driven by an insatiable desire to be successful and operated on the principal, "Lead, follow, or get out of the way." This is a problem in any given situation but is exacerbated when you are leading a group of volunteers. I had been accused of being angry, and I'm sure I was at times, but the need for achievement was driving everything. The problem was that success was defined by my own need to be accepted by those who were important to me. I needed to be successful in their eyes at any cost.*

*Through taking the evaluation I have been able to bring the need of acceptance and success into line with the direction the Lord has defined for me, and I am much better prepared and able to succeed at His calling rather than be a success at my own definition. There was never a down moment in my definition of success, and the evaluation has helped me see this is wrong thinking and helped me to find a place of rest.*

There was no anger in Barry. He was just so driven to achieve that without even noticing it, his blind ambition would run right over his wife. And what he believed would cause her to respect him and would give him the wherewithal to be able to give her anything her heart desired, she viewed as anger.

## LINDSAY'S STORY

Lindsay is a bundle of excitement. She always seems to be optimistic, but privately she has her downs, and they are indeed that . . . down! Her search for something to understand her inner battles was forever on her mind. When she thought there was an answer, it turned not to be *the* answer. We have sat and talked often both formally and informally. But in the course of writing this manuscript, I would share some of my findings with a small group she attended. After the group dismissed one evening, Lindsay asked to take the evaluation. I will let her respond to her results:

*About a year ago, I committed myself to forsake my casual Christianity and launch into a sincere intimate relationship with Christ. I needed to be so close to Christ that my spiritual ears were perpetually tuned to*

Him. *I wanted my thoughts to be His thoughts, my will to be His will, my emotions to be His emotions.*

*I wanted to know why I was constantly struggling with anger, gluttony, and bouts of self-criticizing and depression. What was I missing? What was keeping me from aligning with God?*

*I took my time filling in the survey. I wanted to be honest about my answers. I admit the results puzzled me at first, but after reviewing my primary hunger with Dr. Ledbetter, I came to understand myself and was empowered to make the necessary changes.*

*The resulting numbers revealed the main hungers I was trying to feed, without feeling satisfied. My top score, thirteen, was in the category of excitement, ecstasy, and delight. According to the hunger evaluation, I hungered for happiness. That surprised me. I considered myself to be a happy person most of the time. I found delight in many ways. I am delighted when my husband is pleased. I am delighted when our son succeeds. I am delighted when I trigger someone to smile. I am delighted when I am eating anything delicious. I asked, "With so many ways to satisfy my hunger for happiness, why is it my top hunger?"*

*The answer was simple yet illuminating. I was depending on others to feed my hunger for happiness. I realized in that moment I needed to exclusively depend on the Holy Spirit to produce His fruit in me. Joy! God's joy! Unspeakable joy! A joy that is independent of conditions, situations, expectations, and misfortunes. Depending on others to satiate my hunger left me empty and unsatisfied. The fruit of the Holy Spirit is the only nourishment that truly gratifies my hunger.*

## ERIN'S STORY

Erin is a single mom raising four children while maintaining a prestigious occupation. To me, single moms are heroes.

Erin never really shared with me any deep hunger she felt the need to address. I still believe it was her curiosity about the hunger evaluation that prompted her to ask if she could take it. So I gave her an evaluation with the promise she would let me see it.

Following is Erin's response. It fascinated me. If you knew her it would probably intrigue you too.

*The hunger evaluation revealed a side of me I really didn't expect to see. The hunger I was feeding was achievement. I was shocked and bothered by the result, and at first I rejected it. I fixated on the negative aspect of this hunger. However, later I understood it was in fact very true. I've been accused of being a workaholic, and sometimes, even though I don't want to admit it, I know this accusation is correct. But I don't want it to be. My children and my family are more important to me, yet fulfilling this hunger tended to rob me of precious time when I could be with them.*

*The solutions that the works of the flesh offered seemed too farfetched to be true. I certainly didn't see myself seeking fulfillment through envy or murder. That was when it dawned on me that there are ways to kill other than the physical. We can kill love. We can kill someone's reputation. We can kill excitement in the heart of our children, and my hunger for achievement had the possibility of doing that.*

*God, through the fruit of the Spirit, offers gentleness. I immediately knew what I had to do and which direction I needed to take.*

## PATRICK'S STORY

Patrick called my office and asked for an appointment. We had met many times before, but this time it was a lunch appointment, and he was buying. When he picked me up and took me to a familiar local restaurant, it wasn't for small talk or pleasantries, it was deeper . . . much deeper. He had lost his wife of forty years to an awful disease four months prior. When it was her time, she went fast. There is no handbook for what to say during times like these, so I just listened. His dreadful loneliness was obvious. As I walked out of the building, I hoped that somehow I might have been some comfort and a measure of encouragement.

As I was getting in his car, Patrick asked if he could stop by my office and take the hunger evaluation. He had heard how it had helped others identify where their focus should be in order to navigate their situation. So we headed back to the office where I retrieved one from my desk files, handed it to him, and asked him to email me his results. He did, and his understandable hunger for intimacy came as no surprise. I could have told him that before he took the evaluation, but I wanted him to see the results of his answers for himself. His hunger was on evident display in black and white right in front of him.

We had a conversation as to where the flesh will likely taunt him in the near future. One look at the hunger matrix, and he saw where his battle would be; in fact, it had already begun. So we talked about how he needed to seek the ubiquitous *agape* love available at such a time as this in his life. The Holy Spirit will produce it in him at the point of his surrender.

He agreed.

## TANYA'S STORY

Tanya has been married only for the time it takes for two quick offspring to arrive. She, her husband, and babies are a beautiful family. Tanya thinks she wants to be connected, and her sanguine personality tells everyone around that she is. But down deep it's intimacy she desires. The short life of a manufactured happiness circumvents true lasting connection. From where does real intimacy come? After taking the evaluation, Tanya sent me this note. I asked if I could share it with you:

> *Knowing that my soul's hunger is intimacy has really helped me stay on track with my relationship with God as well as my marriage. Whenever I am feeling not heard or unappreciated, instead of running to someone else for temporary love and attention, I run to God and ask Him to show me His love and help build me back up into a whole heart again. Before finding out my soul's hunger, I had been trying to connect more with others and trying to find love from people who could not help fix me permanently . . . only temporarily. Now knowing what I need to feel satisfied is having a deeper connection with God, I spend more time in prayer and journaling to make sure I am fixing and building back up the broken pieces inside me that cannot be fixed with the works of the flesh but only by the fruit of the Spirit!*

## INDISTINCTNESS CREATES INDECISIVENESS

My hope is that the time you have taken to discover how the hunger evaluation can work for you will be profitable. Since it is true that the flesh wars daily against the Spirit, it is my desire that you now will be able to put a face on the enemy with whom you may be warring. A fierce battle requires certainty. And it is my fear that many believers in the middle of a brutal spiritual battle are confused as to who or what the enemy really is, and because of hesitation are suffering loss.

Don't let that be you!

After you have taken the evaluation, saturate your mind with the Scriptures provided for you. Name the hunger. Name the rogue fake substitutes put in place and manipulated by Satan. Name the real fruit of the Spirit that God provides to help you get resolution. Face the counterfeits, the surrogates, the phonies, and stare the cowards down.

*To help you solidify this process, after submitting to the evaluation, answer these important questions:*

1. What hunger are you presently trying to feed?

_____

_____

_____

2. What works of the flesh that will feed this hunger do you need to avoid?

_____

_____

_____

3. How would you define how they may work against you in this present situation?

_____

_____

_____

_____

_____

4. Write out a few Scripture passages that will help in this battle.

_____

_____

_____

_____

_____

5. Which aspect of the fruit of the Spirit might God use to better satisfy your hunger?

_____

_____

_____

_____

_____

6. Is there one particular Scripture that encouraged you today? Write it down:

_____

_____

_____

_____

7. Name a friend to share outcomes with. Write down what you might share with them about your battle.

_____

_____

_____

_____

_____

# Appendix: Scripture Concerning Each Hunger

## Three List Matrix

| The Works of the Flesh | The Hunger | The Fruit of the Spirit |
|---|---|---|
| Adultery/Fornication | Intimacy | Love |
| Uncleanness/Lewdness | Happiness | Joy |
| Idolatry/Sorcery | Contentment | Peace |
| Hatred/Contentions | Justice | Longsuffering |
| Jealousies/Anger | Control | Kindness |
| Selfish Ambitions/Dissensions | Respect | Goodness |
| Heresies ("My Truth") | Truth | Faithfulness |
| Envy/Murders | Achievement | Gentleness |
| Drunkenness/Revelries | Pleasure | Self-Control |

## Chapter Two: The Hunger for Intimacy

**The Hunger: Intimacy**

Introduction: The human hunger for intimacy—connection, closeness, togetherness, affinity, friendship—is present because God designed us to need each other: "And the LORD God said, 'It is not good that man should be alone'" (Genesis 2:18).

Isaiah 41:10
Matthew 28:20

Romans 12:5
Romans 12:10
Romans 15:7
Romans 15:14
Galatians 5:13
Galatians 6:2
Ephesians 5:21
Colossians 3:13
1 Thessalonians 5:11
Hebrews 13:5

## Works of the Flesh: Adultery/Fornication

1. Biblical teaching about sexual immorality.
   1 Corinthians 5:1–5
   1 Corinthians 6:13
   1 Corinthians 6:18
   2 Corinthians 12:21
   Ephesians 5:3
   1 Thessalonians 4:3
   Revelation 2:21

2. How is sexual immorality overcome?
   Genesis 39:7–9, 12
   Job 31:1
   Psalm 51:10
   Psalm 101:3
   Psalm 119:37
   Proverbs 4:23
   Proverbs 27:20
   Mark 7:21
   Romans 12:1
   1 Corinthians 6:18–20
   1 Corinthians 10:13
   2 Corinthians 10:4–5
   Philippians 4:8
   Colossians 3:2

**Fruit of the Spirit: Love**

1. Does God really love you?
   John 3:16
   Romans 5:8
   1 John 4:9–11

2. How should I show my love to God?
   John 14:15
   John 14:21–23
   2 John 6

3. How can I love people I don't even like?
   John 13:34–35
   1 Peter 4:8
   1 John 2:9–10
   1 John 4:9

4. How does this divine love in me grow? Can we pursue it?
   2 Timothy 2:22
   1 John 4:7–8
   2 Peter 1:5–9
   Revelation 2:4–5

**Scripture about Love (*Agape*)**

Luke 10:27—So he answered and said, "'You shall love the LORD your God with all your heart, with all your soul, with all your strength, and with all your mind,' and 'your neighbor as yourself.'"

John 3:16—For God so loved the world that He gave His only begotten Son, that whoever believes in him should not perish but have everlasting life.

John 15:13—Greater love has no one than this, than to lay down one's life for his friends.

Romans 5:8—But God demonstrates His own love toward us, in that while we were still sinners, Christ died for us.

1 Corinthians 13:7—[Love] bears all things, believes all things, hopes all things, endures all things.

Colossians 3:14—But above all these things put on love, which is the bond of perfection.

1 John 4:7—Beloved, let us love one another: for love is of God; and everyone who loves is born of God and knows God.

1 John 4:18—There is no fear in love; but perfect love casts out fear, because fear involves torment. But he who fears has not been made perfect in love.

1 John 4:10—In this is love, not that we loved God, but that He loved us and sent His Son to be the propitiation for our sins.

# CHAPTER THREE:
# THE HUNGER FOR HAPPINESS

**The Hunger: Happiness**

Introduction: Happiness is a derivative of other things we experience, achieve, or choose. When we are pursuing happiness, we are actually saying we are looking for things that will produce happiness. These might be things to explore or achieve, but happiness will only be found in the ultimate relationship. "More than that, blessed [happy] are those who hear the word of God and keep it!" (Luke 11:28).

Deuteronomy 33:29
2 Chronicles 9:7
Job 5:17
Psalm 37:4–14
Psalm 144:15
Matthew 5:8
1 Peter 4:13

**Works of the Flesh: Uncleanness/Lewdness**

1. The combination of these two words *uncleanness* and *lewdness* is hedonism. Antonyms for lewdness are: lascivious, licentious, lustful, salacious, and wanton.

2 Corinthians 12:21

2. Why is there uncleanness and lewdness?
Mark 7:22–23
Ephesians 4:19
Romans 1:24
Jude 4

3. How can I eliminate uncleanness and lewdness?
   Romans 13:14
   Ephesians 5:3
   Colossians 3:5
   2 Corinthians 12:21
   1 Peter 4:3

**Fruit of the Spirit: Joy**

1. Where does joy come from, and how do I cultivate it in my life?
   Jeremiah 15:16
   Psalm 4:7
   Psalm 16:11
   Psalm 43:4
   Psalm 51:12
   John 15:11
   John 16:24
   Romans 12:12
   Philippians 1:25
   Hebrews 12:11
   Hebrews 12:2
   1 Peter 1:8
   1 John 1:4
   2 John 12

2. What motivation should I have to choose joy?
   John 16:20
   1 Thessalonians 5:16–18
   James 1:2–3

3. How should I deal with "joy-suckers"?
   1 Samuel 1:1–10
   1 Samuel 2:1–2

4. But I don't feel joyful. What do I do?
   Psalm 51:12
   Isaiah 61:10
   Luke 10:20b
   Philippians 4:4
   James 1:2–3

### Scripture about Joy

Psalm 16:11—You will show me the path of life; in Your presence *is* fullness of joy; at Your right hand are pleasures forevermore.

Psalm 119:111—Your testimonies I have taken as a heritage forever, for they are the rejoicing of my heart.

Psalm 149:4—For the LORD takes pleasure in His people; He will beautify the humble with salvation.

Proverbs 15:23—A man has joy by the answer of his mouth, and a word spoken in due season, how good it is!

Isaiah 61:10—I will greatly rejoice in the LORD, My soul shall be joyful in my God; for He has clothed me with the garments of salvation, He has covered me with the robe of righteousness, as a bridegroom decks himself with ornaments, and as a bride adorns herself with her jewels.

John 16:24—Until now you have asked nothing in My name. Ask, and you will receive, that your joy may be full.

Romans 15:32—That I may come to you with joy by the will of God, and may be refreshed together with you.

2 Corinthians 12:10—Therefore I take pleasure in infirmities, in reproaches, in needs, in persecutions, in distresses, for Christ's sake. For when I am weak, then am I strong.

1 Timothy 6:17—Command those who are rich in this present age not to be haughty, nor to trust in uncertain riches but in the living God, who gives us richly all things to enjoy.

1 Peter 1:8–9—Whom having not seen you love. Though now you do not see Him, yet believing, you rejoice with joy inexpressible and full of glory, receiving the end of your faith—the salvation of your souls.

## CHAPTER FOUR: THE HUNGER FOR CONTENTMENT

### The Hunger: Contentment

Introduction: Jesus summed up contentment by leaving His disciples with these three powerful heartening contemplations found in John 14:27: *I want you peaceful!* "Peace I leave with you." Not the absence of conflict, but an underlying contentment that generates an unspeakable peace. *I want you untroubled!* "Let not your heart be troubled." *I want you unafraid!* "Neither let [your heart] be afraid." "Not that I speak in regard to need, for I have learned in whatever state I am, to be content" (Philippians 4:11).

Ecclesiastes 5:10
Psalm 37:16
Isaiah 55:2

## Works of the Flesh: Idolatry/Sorcery

Isaiah 59:8
Ezekiel 14:3–4
Ephesians 5:5
Philippians 3:19
Colossians 3:5
1 Corinthians 10:14
1 Corinthians 10:19–20
1 John 5:21

## Fruit of the Spirit: Peace

Isaiah 26:3
John 14:27
Romans 8:6
Ephesians 2:13–14
Philippians 4:7
Colossians 3:15

1. What aspects about peace does the Bible teach?
Peace with Myself
Genesis 1:27
Psalm 139
Isaiah 45:9–10
Peace with God
Romans 5:1
Ephesians 2:14
Colossians 1:20
Peace of God
Romans 15:33
2 Corinthians 13:11
Philippians 4:4–7
1 Thessalonians 5:23
2 Thessalonians 3:16

2. How can I choose peace?
   Psalm 119:165
   Isaiah 26:3
   John 16:33
   Romans 8:6
   Romans 12:1
   Galatians 5:22
   Philippians 4:4–7

## Scripture about Peace

Psalm 4:8—I will both lie down in peace, and sleep; for You alone, O LORD, make me dwell in safety.

Proverbs 12:20—Deceit is in the heart of those who devise evil, but counselors of peace have joy.

Isaiah 26:3—You will keep him in perfect peace, whose mind is stayed on You, because he trusts in You.

John 16:33—These things I have spoken to you, that in Me you may have peace. In the world you will have tribulation; but be of good cheer, I have overcome the world.

Romans 12:18—If it is possible, as much as depends on you, live peaceably with all men.

Romans 15:13—Now may the God of hope fill you with all joy and peace in believing, that you may abound in hope by the power of the Holy Spirit.

1 Corinthians 14:33—For God is not the author of confusion but of peace, as in all churches of the saints.

2 Thessalonians 3:16—Now the Lord of peace Himself give you peace always in every way. The Lord be with you all.

Hebrews 12:14—Pursue peace with all people, and holiness, without which no one will see the Lord.

1 Peter 3:11—Let him turn away from evil and do good; let him seek peace and pursue it.

1 Peter 5:7—Casting all your care upon Him, for He cares for you.

# CHAPTER FIVE: THE HUNGER FOR JUSTICE

## The Hunger: Justice

Introduction: Justice comes from the Chief Justice, the creator of the laws of nature, or what we call natural law. Defined, the natural law is a moral theory, which asserts there is a moral code that applies to all humans and which exists within our nature. This moral code is knowable through human reason by reflecting rationally on our nature and purpose as human beings. "To do righteousness and justice is more acceptable to the LORD than sacrifice" (Proverbs 21:3).

Proverbs 11:1
Ecclesiastes 5:8
Micah 6:8

## Works of the Flesh: Hatred/Contentions

1 Corinthians 3:3
Ephesians 2:12–14

1. Caused by:
   Proverbs 10:12
   Proverbs 13:10; 28:25
   Proverbs 15:18; 30:33
   Proverbs 16:27–28; 26:21
   Proverbs 23:29–30
   Proverbs 26:20
   1 Timothy 6:4
   2 Timothy 2:14, 23
   James 3:16
   James 4:1

2. Don't be contentious:
   Proverbs 20:3
   Romans 13:13
   Philippians 2:14

## Fruit of the Spirit: Longsuffering

Proverbs 15:18
Romans 15:5

Ephesians 4:2
(Notice how all components of the fruit of the Spirit work together).
Colossians 1:11

1. Longsuffering/Patience is a command from God:
   1 Thessalonians 5:14
   James 1:4
   2 Peter 1:5–7

2. Problems and trials lead to longsuffering/patience:
   Romans 5:3–4
   Hebrews 12:1
   James 1:3–4
   1 Peter 2:20

3. The benefits of longsuffering and waiting on God:
   Psalm 40:1
   Romans 5:4–5

## Scripture about Longsuffering

Exodus 34:6—And the LORD passed before him and proclaimed, "The LORD, the LORD God, merciful and gracious, longsuffering, and abounding in goodness and truth.

John 3:15—That whoever believes in Him should not perish but have eternal life.

Romans 2:4—Or do you despise the riches of His goodness, forbearance, and longsuffering, not knowing that the goodness of God leads you to repentance?

Romans 5:3–4—And not only that, but we also glory in tribulations, knowing that tribulation produces perseverance.

Romans 8:28—And we know that all things work together for good to those who love God, to those who are the called according to His purpose.

Romans 9:22—What if God, wanting to show His wrath and to make His power known, endured with much longsuffering the vessels of wrath prepared for destruction.

Galatians 5:22—But the fruit of the Spirit is love, joy, peace, longsuffering, kindness, goodness, faithfulness.

Ephesians 4:2—With all lowliness and gentleness, with longsuffering, bearing with one another in love.

Colossians 3:12—Therefore, as the elect of God, holy and beloved, put on tender mercies, kindness, humility, meekness, longsuffering.

2 Peter 3:9—The Lord is not slack concerning His promise, as some count slackness, but is longsuffering toward us, not willing that any should perish but that all should come to repentance.

## CHAPTER SIX: THE HUNGER FOR CONTROL

**The Hunger: Control**

Introduction: The answer to who is in charge is key to understanding daily issues of responsibility. This question might formulate itself as: Who pays the consequences? Who is to blame? To whom are we answerable? We seek these answers so persistently because responsibility is an indicator of control, and control is something all of us want. "He who is slow to anger is better than the mighty, and he who rules [controls] his spirit than he who takes a city" (Proverbs 16:32).

> Proverbs 23:7
> Romans 16:17–18
> Galatians 4:17

**Works of the Flesh: Jealousy/Anger**

1. Why do we become jealous?
   Acts 13:45
   Romans 13:13
   1 Corinthians 3:3
   James 3:14–16

2. Why is jealousy harmful?
   Acts 17:5–7

3. Why do I get angry?
   Genesis 4:4–5—Cain
   Numbers 22:29—Balaam
   1 Samuel 18:8—Saul
   2 Chronicles 26:18–19—Uzziah
   Esther 3:5—Haman
   Ecclesiastes 7:9—Fools

4. The Bible repeatedly says to be slow to anger:
   Proverbs 14:29; 15:18; 16:32; 19:11
   Ecclesiastes 7:9

5. When I am angry, why do I need to be especially cautious?
   Proverbs 21:23
   Matthew 12:33–36
   Romans 12:1–2
   James 3:5, 8

**Fruit of the Spirit: Kindness**

1. God's tender concern for others, a nurturing spirit:
   Hosea 11:4
   Zephaniah 3:17

2. God calls us to show this tender concern to others:
   Romans 12:10
   Ephesians 2:6–10
   Titus 3:1–8
   2 Peter 1:7–8

**Scripture on Kindness**

Proverbs 11:17—The merciful man does good for his own soul, but he who is cruel troubles his own flesh.
Proverbs 31:26—She opens her mouth with wisdom, and on her tongue is the law of kindness.
Luke 6:35—But love your enemies, do good, and lend, hoping for nothing in return; and your reward will be great, and you will be sons of the Most High. For He is kind to the unthankful and evil.
1 Corinthians 13:4–7—Love suffers long and is kind; love does not envy; love does not parade itself, is not puffed up.
Galatians 6:10—Therefore, as we have opportunity, let us do good to all, especially to those who are of the household of faith.
Ephesians 4:32—And be kind one to another, tenderhearted, forgiving one another, even as God in Christ forgave you.
Philippians 2:1–3—Therefore if there is any consolation in Christ, if any comfort of love, if any fellowship of the Spirit, if any affection and mercy, fulfill my

joy by being like-minded, having the same love, being of one accord, of one mind. Let nothing be done through selfish ambition or conceit, but in lowliness of mind let each esteem others better than himself.
Colossians 3:12—Therefore, as the elect of God, holy and beloved, put on tender mercies, kindness, humility, meekness, longsuffering.
1 Peter 3:9—Not returning evil for evil or reviling for reviling, but on the contrary blessing, knowing that you were called to this, that you may inherit a blessing.
1 John 3:18—My little children, let us not love in word or in tongue, but in deed and in truth.

## CHAPTER SEVEN: THE HUNGER FOR RESPECT

### The Hunger: Respect

Introduction: *Ethics, etiquette,* and *respect.* Each of these words rests at the core of our existence. Remove them, and you will remove civility from the human race. "Honor [respect] all people. Love the brotherhood. Fear God. Honor [respect] the king" (1 Peter 2:17).

Romans 13:7
1 Thessalonians 5:12
1 Peter 2:18

### Works of the Flesh: Selfish Ambitions/Dissensions

1. Examples of selfish ambition behavior:
   2 Corinthians 12:20
   Philippians 2:3

2. Dissensions are inconsistent with Christian love:
   Romans 12:4–5
   1 Corinthians 10:24
   1 Corinthians 13:5
   2 Corinthians 5:14–15
   Philippians 2:4

3. Dissensions are a natural inclination and characteristic of the last days:
   Ephesians 2:3
   2 Timothy 3:1–2

**Fruit of the Spirit: Goodness**

1. The word occurs three other times in the New Testament besides Galatians 5:
   Romans 15:14
   Ephesians 5:9
   2 Thessalonians 1:11
2. Goodness results from uprightness of heart:
   Proverbs 3:7
   Proverbs 15:3
   Proverbs 15:33
   1 John 3:3

3. In the New Testament, kindness (previous chapter) and goodness (this chapter) frequently team up—it is as though they were two sides of the same coin.
   Ephesians 2:7, 10
   Titus 3:4, 7–8

Notice again the sequencing of each aspect of the fruit of the Holy Spirit in the life of the believer: love + joy + peace + patience + kindness proceed goodness.

**Scripture on Goodness**

Psalm 23:6—Surely goodness and mercy shall follow me all the days of my life; and I will dwell in the house of the LORD forever.
Psalm 27:13—I would have lost heart, unless I had believed that I would see the goodness of the LORD in the land of the living.
Psalm 31:19—Oh, how great is Your goodness, which You have laid up for those who fear You, which You have prepared for those who trust in You in the presence of the sons of men!
Psalm 34:8—Oh, taste and see that the LORD is good: blessed is the man who trusts in Him!
Micah 6:8—He has shown you, O man, what is good; and what does the LORD require of you but to do justly, to love mercy, and to walk humbly with your God?
Matthew 12:35—A good man out of the good treasure of his heart brings forth good things, and an evil man out of the evil treasure brings forth evil things.
Romans 8:28—And we know that all things work together for good to those who love God, to those who are the called according to His purpose.
Romans 12:9—Let love be without hypocrisy. Abhor what is evil. Cling to what is good.

Galatians 5:22—But the fruit of the Spirit is love, joy, peace, longsuffering, kindness, goodness, faithfulness.

James 1:17—Every good gift and every perfect gift is from above, and comes down from the Father of lights, with whom is no variation or shadow of turning.

James 3:13— Who is wise and understanding among you? Let him show by good conduct that his works are done in the meekness of wisdom.

Galatians 6:10—As we have therefore opportunity, let us do good unto all, especially to those who are of the household of faith.

## CHAPTER EIGHT: THE HUNGER FOR TRUTH

### The Hunger: Truth

Introduction: The hunger for truth resides deeply within us. Perhaps there is something deep within you even as your eyes pass over this sentence for which you crave the truth. With the rampant deception in the public arena of the world, no wonder we are so hungry. God put that truth hunger inside us. "And you shall know the truth, and the truth shall make you free" (John 8:32).

Psalm 33:4
John 4:24
John 14:6
John 15:26–27
1 John 1:6
1 John 3:18

### Work of the Flesh: Heresies

Galatians 1:6–7
Hebrews 13:9
2 Peter 2:1

### Fruit of the Spirit: Faithfulness

1. The degree of our faithfulness is the direct result of our regard for God's faithfulness:
Exodus 34:1–6
Lamentations 3:22–23
Psalm 145:13

2. Faithfulness is making faith a living reality in one's life:
   Proverbs 20:6
   1 Corinthians 4:2

3. Consistency: Developing an intentional, conscious, obedience to God's Word.
   John 14:15
   John 15:10
   1 Peter 4:19

4. How to live out convictions:
   Daniel 1:8
   Daniel 3:16–18
   Psalm 119:7
   Psalm 143:8

4. The world crowns success, but God crowns faithfulness:
   Psalm 27:8
   2 Corinthians 5:7
   Ephesians 6:16
   Hebrews 11:6

5. The dangers of "little faith":
   Matthew 6:30—Anxiety
   Hebrews 10:38—Timidity
   Matthew 14:31—Doubt
   Matthew 16:8–12—Lack Understanding

6. How do we increase our faith, hence our faithfulness?
   Hebrews 11
   Romans 10:17
   Revelation 3:20

### Scripture on Faithfulness

Psalm 89:33—Nevertheless My lovingkindness I will not utterly take from him, nor allow My faithfulness to fail.

Proverbs 3:3–4—Let not mercy and truth forsake you; bind them about your neck, write them on the tablet of your heart.

Proverbs 28:20—A faithful man will abound with blessings, but he who hastens to be rich will not go unpunished.

Luke 12:42–44—And the Lord said, "Who then is that faithful and wise steward, whom his master will make ruler over his household, to give them their portion of food in due season?

Luke 16:10—He who is faithful in what is least is faithful also in much; and he who is unjust in what is least is unjust also in much.

John 14:15—If you love Me, keep My commandments.

1 Corinthians 10:13—No temptation has overtaken you except such as is common to man; but God is faithful, who will not allow you to be tempted beyond what you are able, but with the temptation will also make the way of escape, that you may be able to bear it.

2 Corinthians 5:7—For we walk by faith, not by sight.

Galatians 5:22—But the fruit of the Spirit is love, joy, peace, longsuffering, kindness, goodness, faithfulness.

2 Timothy 2:13—If we are faithless, He remains faithful; He cannot deny Himself.

1 John 1:9—If we confess our sins, He is faithful and just to forgive our sins and to cleanse us from all unrighteousness.

1 Corinthians 4:2—Moreover it is required in stewards that one be found faithful.

# CHAPTER NINE: THE HUNGER FOR ACHIEVEMENT

### The Hunger: Achievement

Introduction: The human hunger for achievement. What utterly satisfies our hunger for achievement is not the achievements themselves, but knowing they have been pursued according to gentleness. "Your gentleness has made me great" (Psalm 18:35).

Ecclesiastes 9:10
1 Corinthians 9:24–27
Philippians 4:13
Hebrews 10:35–36

## Works of the Flesh: Envy/ Murders

Envy:
Matthew 27:18
1 Timothy 6:3–4

Murder:
Proverbs 26:24–25
Ezekiel 22:9, 12–13
Matthew 5:21
Romans 1:28-32
1 John 3:15

## Fruit of the Spirit: Gentleness

1. Gentleness is strength under control, used of a horse responsive to the bridle.
Matthew 5:5
Matthew 11:29–30
2 Corinthians 10:1
Galatians 6:1
Ephesians 4:1–3
Colossians 3:12
1 Timothy 6:11
2 Timothy 2:24–25
Titus 3:1–2
1 Peter 2:21–23

2. Gentleness is an essential quality:
2 Timothy 2:25—In teaching others
James 1:21—To receive the Word of God
James 3:13—To our assurance

3. Promises given to the gentle:
Psalm 25:9
Psalm 37:11
Isaiah 29:19
Matthew 5:5

### Scripture on Gentleness

2 Samuel 22:36—You have also given me the shield of Your salvation; Your gentleness has made me great.

Psalm 18:35—You have also given me the shield of Your salvation; Your right hand has held me up, Your gentleness has made me great.

Proverbs 15:1—A soft answer turns away wrath, but a harsh word stirs up anger.

Isaiah 40:11—He will feed His flock like a shepherd; He will gather the lambs with His arm, and carry them in His bosom, and gently lead those who are with young.

Matthew 11:29—Take My yoke upon you and learn from Me, for I am gentle and lowly in heart, and you will find rest for your souls.

1 Corinthians 13:4–5—Love suffers long and is kind; love does not envy; love does not parade itself, is not puffed up.

Galatians 5:22–23—But the fruit of the Spirit is love, joy, peace, longsuffering, kindness, goodness, faithfulness, gentleness, self-control.

Galatians 6:1—Brethren, if a man is overtaken in any trespass, you who are spiritual restore such a one in a spirit of gentleness, considering yourself lest you also be tempted.

Ephesians 4:2—With all lowliness and gentleness, with longsuffering, bearing with one another in love.

2 Timothy 2:24—And a servant of the Lord must not quarrel but be gentle to all, able to teach, patient.

Titus 3:1–2—Remind them to be subject to rulers and authorities, to obey, to be ready for every good work, to speak evil of no one, to be peaceable, gentle, showing all humility to all men.

James 1:19–20—So then, my beloved brethren, let every man be swift to hear, slow to speak, slow to wrath; for the wrath of man does not produce the righteousness of God.

James 3:17—But the wisdom that is from above is first pure, then peaceable, gentle, willing to yield, full of mercy and good fruits, without partiality and without hypocrisy.

1 Peter 3:15—But sanctify the Lord God in your hearts, and always be ready to give a defense to everyone who asks you a reason for the hope that is in you, with meekness and fear.

# CHAPTER TEN: THE HUNGER FOR PLEASURE

### The Hunger: Pleasure

Introduction: Certainly there are some off-limit pleasures, but the restriction of the general idea of pleasure, and even seeking it, is nowhere even in a sentence contained in the Bible. King David says that joy to the full and everlasting pleasures are found in God's presence. "You will show me the path of life; in Your presence is fullness of joy; at Your right hand are pleasures forevermore" (Psalm 16:11).

Seeking pleasures will never satisfy:
Ecclesiastes 1:1–11
Ecclesiastes 2:12–26
Ecclesiastes 5:10–20

### Works of the Flesh: Drunkenness/Revelries

Luke 21:34–35
Romans 13:13–14
Ephesians 5:18
1 Peter 4:3

1. Can God help me overcome my addictions?
   1 Corinthians 10:13
   2 Corinthians 5:17

2. "I like my habit; I can handle it! Of course I'm not addicted!"
   John 8:34
   Romans 6:12, 16
   2 Peter 2:19

### Fruit of the Spirit: Temperance

1. Temperance/self-control is the control of passions and appetites.
   1 Corinthians 7:9
   1 Corinthians 9:25
   2 Peter 1:5–8

2. Why can't I control certain desires?
   Romans 7:15–25

Romans 12:1
Romans 13:14

3. What steps are useful for exercising temperance/self-control?
Psalm 119:9
Proverbs 13:3
Matthew 12:34–37
Romans 8:6
1 Corinthians 6:12; 10:23, 31
1 Timothy 4:8
James 1:26
James 3:1–12

## Scripture on Temperance

Proverbs 25:26—A righteous man who falters before the wicked is like a murky spring and a polluted well.

Proverbs 25:28—Whoever has no rule over his own spirit is like a city broken down, without walls.

Romans 12:19—Beloved, do not avenge yourselves, but rather give place to wrath; for it is written, "Vengeance *is* Mine, I will repay," says the Lord.

Galatians 5:23—Gentleness, self-control. Against such there is no law.

2 Timothy 1:7—For God has not given us a spirit of fear, but of power and of love and of a sound mind.

Titus 1:8—But hospitable, a lover of what is good, sober-minded, just, holy, self-controlled.

Titus 2:6—Likewise, exhort the young men to be sober-minded.

1 Peter 4:7—But the end of all things is at hand; therefore be serious and watchful in your prayers.

James 1:20—For the wrath of man does not produce the righteousness of God.

1 Peter 5:8—Be sober, be vigilant; because your adversary the devil walks about like a roaring lion, seeking whom he may devour.

2 Peter 1:5—But also for this very reason, giving all diligence, add to your faith virtue, to virtue knowledge.

I awake early. My mind rushes in filled with anxiety over issues in my life,
in my children's lives . . . I look to Him!

Today I choose:

## LOVE

Nothing I am going through allows me to hate. I love because He loves me.

## JOY

May God give me eyes to see through to the heart
of people and not their actions or words.

## PEACE

Father, forgive my mistakes and sins. Thank you for your forgiveness!
Help me to forgive others.

## LONGSUFFERING

You, Lord, have been so patient with me. Please don't give up on me.
Help me to be patient with *all* around me.

## KINDNESS

Thank you for the examples of kindness you give me.
In all circumstances, help me be kind.

## GOODNESS

In every way, in every day, show me ways to be good whether there is a need or not.
(Even if someone is not good to me!)

## FAITHFULNESS

Let me speak truth! Let my word be always true. Your name is
worth so much more to me than all the riches of this world.

## GENTLENESS

To those I know and love, let me be gentle. To those I don't know
or those who may not even like me, let me be gentle.

## SELF-CONTROL

Never let me offend. Control my tongue, my actions, and my thoughts!
Build up. Don't tear down. Speak through me.

Please Father, help the fruit of the Spirit describe my day. Help it define who I am.
I commit to these things and to having them become real, relevant,
and an innate part of my daily life.

*Janet Seibert, 2019*

**If you enjoyed this book, will you consider sharing the message with others?**

Let us know your thoughts at info@newhopepublishers.com. You can also let the author know by visiting or sharing a photo of the cover on our social media pages or leaving a review at a retailer's site. All of it helps us get the message out!

Twitter.com/NewHopeBooks

Facebook.com/NewHopePublishers

Instagram.com/NewHopePublishers

———————

New Hope® Publishers is an imprint of Iron Stream Media,
which derives its name from Proverbs 27:17,
"As iron sharpens iron, so one person sharpens another."

This sharpening describes the process of discipleship, one to another. With this in mind, Iron Stream Media provides a variety of solutions for churches, missionaries, and nonprofits ranging from in-depth Bible study curriculum and Christian book publishing to custom publishing and consultative services. Through the popular Life Bible Study and Student Life Bible Study brands, ISM provides web-based full-year and short-term Bible study teaching plans as well as printed devotionals, Bibles, and discipleship curriculum.

For more information on ISM and New Hope Publishers, please visit

IronStreamMedia.com

NewHopePublishers.com

# Other Spiritual Growth
# RESOURCES

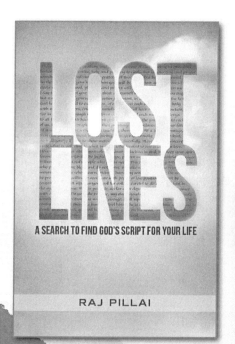

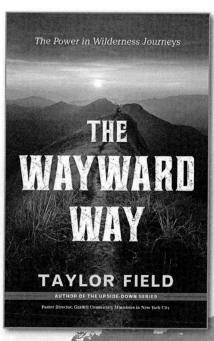